SALT-WATER TROPICAL FISH in your home

By GAIL CAMPBELL

S STERLING
PUBLISHING CO., INC. NEW YORK

Oak Tree Press Co., Ltd. London & Sydney

OTHER BOOKS OF INTEREST

Color Guide to Tropical Fish
Guppy: Its Life Cycle
Marine Aquarium Fish Identifier
Naturalists' Guide to Fresh-Water Aquarium Fish
Oddball Fishes & Other Strange Creatures of the Deep
Siamese Fighting Fish: Its Life Cycle
Tropical Fish Identifier
Tropical Fish in Your Home

Copyright © 1976 by Gail Campbell

Published by Sterling Publishing Co., Inc.
419 Park Avenue South, New York, N.Y. 10016
Distributed in Australia and New Zealand by Oak Tree Press Co., Ltd.,
P.O. Box J34, Brickfield Hill, Sydney 2000, N.S.W.
Distributed in the United Kingdom and elsewhere in the British Commonwealth
by Ward Lock Ltd., 116 Baker Street, London W 1
Manufactured in the United States of America
All rights reserved
Library of Congress Catalog Card No.: 76–1175
Sterling ISBN 0-8069-3730–0 Trade   Oak Tree 7061-2167–8
3731–9 Library

Contents

Foreword 7

Glossary 9

Introduction 11

1. Equipment for the Salt-Water Aquarium 13
   Type of Tank to Start With . . . Larger Size Tanks
   Preferred . . . Where to Locate Your Tank . . . Hood and
   Light . . . Kind of Sand . . . Subsand Filter . . . Outside
   Filter . . . Ultraviolet Light for Purification . . . Aeration

2. The Water Itself 20
   Synthetic Versus Natural Sea Water . . . Collecting Sea
   Water . . . Heating the Water . . . Setting Up an Isolation
   Tank

3. Setting Up a Successful Aquarium 24

4. Selecting and Maintaining Fishes 26
   Planning and Choosing Marine Fishes . . . Tank Capacity
   . . . Conditioning Period . . . Selecting Healthy Fishes
   . . . Feeding . . . Aquarium Maintenance

5. A Stable Environment 33
   Temperature . . . Salinity . . . pH . . . Nitrites

6. Diseases of Marine Fishes 35
   Stress . . . Preventive Medicine . . . Symptoms of Disease
   . . . Parasites . . . Protozoans . . . Bacterial Infections . . .
   Viral Infections . . . Fungus . . . Parasitic Worms . . .
   Parasitic Crustaceans . . . Gas Bubble Disease . . . Popeye
   . . . Tank Sterilization . . . Parts of a Fish . . . Incompata-
   bility Chart

7. Suitable Species for Your Aquarium 48
   Angelfishes—Family Chaetodontidae 48
   Butterflyfishes—Family Chaetodontidae 52
   Surgeonfishes or Tangs—Family Acanthuridae . . . 56
   Moorish Idol—Family Zanclidae 60
   Anemonefishes—Family Pomacentridae 61
   Damselfishes—Family Pomacentridae 63
   Wrasses—Family Labridae 98
   Lionfishes or Scorpionfishes—Family Scorpaenidae . . 102

Triggerfishes—Family Balistidae 103
Filefishes—Family Monocanthidae 107
Puffers—Family Tetraodontidae 108
Trunkfishes—Family Ostraciidae 109
Porcupinefishes and Burrfishes—Family Diodontidae . 111
Squirrelfishes—Family Holocentridae 113
Cardinalfishes—Family Apogonidae 114
Dragonets—Family Callionymidae 115
Gobies—Family Gobiidae 116
Batfishes—Family Platacidae 118
Spadefishes—Family Ephippidae 119
Groupers and Seabasses—Family Serranidae . . . 120
Basslets—Family Grammidae 121
Grunts—Family Pomadasyidae 121
Sweetlips—Family Pomadasyidae 122
Hawkfishes—Family Cirrhitidae 123
Scats—Family Scatophagidae 124
Jawfishes—Family Opistognathidae 124
Catfishes—Family Plotosidae 125
Seahorses and Pipefishes—Family Syngnathidae . . 125
Moray Eels—Family Muraenidae 128
8. Marine Invertebrates for the Aquarium 129
Feeding . . . Sea Anemones . . . Coral . . . Flame Scallop
. . . Hermit Crabs . . . Arrow Crab . . . Banded Coral
Shrimp . . . Sea Stars
9. Breeding Marine Fishes 134
Anemonefishes . . . Damselfishes . . . Seahorses and Pipe-
fishes . . . Gobies
Scientific Name Index 139
Popular Name Index 141
Subject Index 143

ACKNOWLEDGMENTS

The author's sincere thanks are extended to Robert P. Dempster, Curator Emeritus of the Steinhart Aquarium, San Francisco, California, who read the manuscript and provided valuable information for the chapter on diseases, and for the Incompatibility Chart, and to Dr. John E. McCosker, Superintendent of the Steinhart Aquarium, for reading portions of the manuscript and assisting with numerous taxonomical questions.

All of the color photographs, other than those of fish in the author's aquariums, were taken with permission by the author at the following locations: Steinhart Aquarium, California Academy of Sciences, Golden Gate Park, San Francisco, Ca.; Marineland of the Pacific, Palos Verdes, Ca.; Sea World, San Diego, Ca.; T. Wayland Vaughan Aquarium, Scripps Institute of Oceanography, San Diego, Ca.

The author's deepest gratitude is extended to these fine institutions for the use of their displays and for the education and enjoyment they provide for us all.

The author is also indebted to the following people and institutions for the black-and-white photographs: Dr. Herbert R. Axelrod for Beau Gregory, Israeli Puffer, Long-Jawed Squirrelfish; Eugene G. Danner Mfg. Co. Inc., 1660 Summerfield St., Brooklyn, N.Y. 11227, for the power filter; H. Hansen, Aquarium Berlin, for Neon Goby; M. Kocar for Pantherfish; G. Marcuse for Long-Horned Cowfish, Humu-Humu; K. Parpan for Spanish Hogfish, Spiny Boxfish; and G. J. M. Timmerman for Sergeant Major.

Foreword

Colorful exotic marine fishes gracefully swimming and cavorting in a beautifully decorated aquarium are delightful to behold. A feeling of profound joy and a sense of great satisfaction are experienced by the aquarist who is successful in setting up an exhibit such as this in his home. Since the quality of artificial sea water has been vastly improved within the past few years it is now possible for people living inland, who do not have access to natural sea water, to maintain marine aquariums in their homes.

There are of course some problems involved in caring for fishes that are confined in small aquariums. Since the fishes are collected from the oceans, where they have an unlimited area in which to swim and forage for food, they undergo some degree of shock when they are transferred to an aquarium, where the area is quite limited. Adjustment to unfamiliar surroundings and to confinement within the four walls of an aquarium is difficult for wild fishes and it is during this adjustment period that they are most vulnerable to disease. Methods of treating various fish diseases have been adequately described in this book.

Miss Campbell has stressed the importance of acquiring the proper aquarium and filter system for marine fishes. She has emphasized the importance of selecting healthy fishes, and fishes that are compatible with each other. Breeding patterns of various species of fishes including sex determination are also discussed. Twenty-seven families including 100 species of fishes have been described and illustrated.

Considerable thought has been given to the selection, care, and description of some exotic marine invertebrates, such as sea anemones, corals, scallops, crabs, and starfishes, that are suitable for a home aquarium.

Miss Campbell's college training included extensive studies in animal behavior and oceanography. She obtained a B.A. degree from the University of Wisconsin and was elected to the Phi Beta Kappa honor society. After graduation she was given a Sea grant Research Assistantship and Fellowship to study oceanography in the graduate school at the University of Wisconsin. She is an accomplished biologist and has held a position as Marine Biologist with the California Department of Fish and Game for several years. Miss Campbell has had many years of practical experience in maintaining marine aquariums in her home. Her formal education and practical experience, as well as an inherent love for marine tropical fishes have more than qualified her as an authority on techniques for the maintenance of tropical marine fishes in the home.

ROBERT P. DEMPSTER
Curator Emeritus
California Academy of Sciences
Steinhart Aquarium

Glossary

Anal fin: the fin posterior to the vent.

Anterior: toward the head.

Autotrophic: self-nourishing.

Barbels: whisker-like sensory projections found on the head of some fishes such as catfishes.

Canine tooth: a long, conical tooth.

Carnivore: an animal that feeds on animal matter.

Caudal fin: the tail fin.

Caudal peduncle: the part of the body between the posterior end of the anal fin and the caudal fin base.

Ciliate: provided with hair-like appendages.

Circumtropical: around the tropics.

Coelenterate: a member of the phylum Coelenterata, e.g. coral, sea anemone, jellyfish, hydroid.

Copepod: a small crustacean in the subclass Copepoda.

Crustacean: a member of the class Crustacea, e.g. lobster, shrimp, crab, brine shrimp.

Denitrify: to convert nitrates into lower compounds.

Dorsal fin: one or two fins on the back and consisting of spines and/or soft rays.

Echinoderm: a marine animal in the phylum Echinodermata, e.g. sea star, sea urchin.

Ectoparasite: an organism living on the exterior of an animal.

Flagellate: having whip-like appendages which serve as swimming organs.

Fluke: a flattened, parasitic, trematode worm.

Gill: the respiratory organ.

Herbivore: an animal that feeds on plant matter.

Heterotrophic: obtaining nourishment from organic matter.

Hybrid: the offspring of a member of one genus, species, etc., mated with another.

Hydrometer: a floating instrument which determines specific gravity.

Invertebrate: a lower animal lacking a spinal column.

Mollusc: a member of the phylum Mollusca which includes shellfishes (other than crustaceans) such as mussels, clams, oysters, whelks, limpets, slugs, snails, etc.

Mouthbreeder: a type of fish that carries its eggs in its mouth until they hatch.

Nauplius: usually the first stage larval form of a crustacean.

Nematocyst: a stinging cell found in sea anemones, etc.

Ocellus: a spot of one color surrounded by a ring of another color.

Omnivore: an animal which feeds on plant and animal matter.

Opercle: an operculum or gill cover.

Ovipositor: an organ which deposits eggs.

Pectoral fins: a pair of fins usually located behind the gill openings.

Pelvic fins: a pair of fins located on the ventral surface anterior to the anus.

pH: a chemical symbol used to express acidity and alkalinity. pH values range from 0 to 14 with 7 indicating neutrality. Numbers below 7 indicate increasing acidity while those above 7 indicate increasing alkalinity.

Plankton: passively floating or weakly swimming aquatic animals and plants.

Posterior: toward the tail.

Soft dorsal: the portion of the dorsal fin which consists of soft rays.

Soft rays: branched or unbranched fin rays which are usually flexible.

Specific gravity: the ratio of the weight of a volume of substance to the weight of an equal volume of a standard unit such as water.

Spine: a fin ray which is rigid and sharp.

Spinous dorsal: the portion of the dorsal fin which consists of spiny rays.

Swim bladder: also called an air bladder. A gas-filled organ located in the body cavity below the vertebrae.

Symbiosis: the living together in close association of two dissimilar organisms. Usually the relationship is advantageous to one or both members.

Ventral fin: a pelvic fin.

Zooplankton: floating or weakly swimming animal life found in water.

Introduction

The salt-water aquarium field has recently undergone great advances. It is now possible to keep exotic marine fishes from all parts of the world in your living room for many years. The hobby is no longer restricted to those aquarists living near the ocean, since artificial salt water has been vastly improved. The use of the artificial mix has reduced the occurrence of sudden outbreaks of disease which often would wipe out an entire tank of fishes in a few days. Today anyone with a little experience in fish keeping can maintain a healthy marine tank.

The aquariums themselves are better constructed now, have few seams to spring leaks, and most of them have no metal parts. Many new products have been designed specifically for marine tanks, and better preventive measures and cures are available for marine diseases.

The variety of marine fishes and interesting invertebrates appearing on the market is continually expanding, and along with vast improvements in shipping and holding techniques have come reduced prices. In addition, many aquarium shops now carry or specialize exclusively in marine species, and this competition is lowering prices. Unfortunately, until we are able to breed marine fishes on a large scale, their prices will never be as low as their fresh-water counterparts. Diving to collect specimens among coral reefs is a time-consuming and hazardous business. Also the losses encountered in transportation of fishes increase prices greatly. For this reason a chapter on breeding marine fishes has been included in this book, even though the field is still in its infancy. If more hobbyists will experiment and publish their findings, the mysteries of breeding these exotic creatures can be unlocked.

A Plexiglas tank with a hood holds specimens safely. The light mounted on top will bring out the colors of the fishes.

1. Equipment for the Salt-Water Aquarium

TYPE OF TANK TO START WITH

The marine aquarist of today can choose a tank from many shapes and sizes without having to rely on the metal frames or braces used a few years ago. Since metal in contact with salt water is highly toxic to marine life, tanks with metal frames must be avoided or the inner seams must be coated with a protective substance such as silicone rubber. Some of the old aquarium cements may also become toxic in salt water and therefore require a protective coating too. It is far safer to purchase one of the new tanks on the market today.

The new salt-water aquariums have no metal parts and are made entirely of glass or Plexiglas glued together with an inert silicone sealant invented in recent years. This excellent sealant is transparent, somewhat elastic, very strong, and now makes possible tanks of several hundred gallons (500 or more litres) capacity. Glass aquariums consist of four sides and a bottom glued together and can be built by the hobbyist. Beginners, however, are encouraged to buy their first marine aquarium to insure that all accessories fit. Custom-designed tanks are available in wood and glass combinations but their viewing area is greatly reduced.

The new Plexiglas variety is far more stylish than glass and has fewer seams to spring leaks. It generally has rounded front edges, a partial top with holes cut for accessories, and can be bought with a matching hood and light fixture.

The greatest disadvantage to Plexiglas is that it scratches easily, and eventually even the most cautious aquarist will brush a piece of coral or rock against the sides when cleaning. Over the years the scratches accumulate, visibility becomes hampered, and the water appears slightly cloudy due to the disfigured tank.

Glass aquariums are less likely to be scratched but are much more expensive than Plexiglas. In the larger tanks (100 gallons—400 litres—or more), distortion is greater in glass than Plexiglas.

LARGER SIZE TANKS PREFERRED

Avoid tanks of less than 25-gallon (100-litre) capacity unless you are only keeping one or two fishes or invertebrates. Marine fishes require more water and dissolved oxygen than their fresh-water counterparts, and overcrowding and pollution are more likely to occur in a small tank than a large one. Waste products will accumulate faster in a small aquarium, and it will require cleaning more frequently regardless of filters. If you intend to keep a large number of specimens, consider buying one large tank rather than many medium-size ones. The expense and main-tenance will be greatly reduced. A large number of medium-size aquariums would only be an advantage if you intend to keep many incompatible species or want to set up experimental tanks.

WHERE TO LOCATE YOUR TANK

The location of the aquarium must be carefully planned to avoid having to disassemble it later for relocation. Avoid sunny windows, radiators, and drafts since a constant water tempera-ture is essential for healthy fishes. A sunny location will foster dense algae growth which is likely to become uncontrollable. Try to choose a room that does not overheat in the summer. In the winter, an aquarium heater with a thermostatic control will help maintain the desired temperature. (More on this later.)

It is also wise to consider the weight of the tank when it is set up. Salt water weighs 8.5 pounds per gallon (1 kilo per litre), so the water alone for a 25-gallon (100-litre) aquarium will weigh 212.5 pounds (100 kilos) and sand and gravel about 30 pounds (14 kilos) more. The total weight of the same tank in Plexiglas would be about 250 pounds (120 kilos). An aquarium this size can only be safely placed on a sturdy table, on shelving fortified with cinder blocks, or on a wrought-iron aquarium stand. For larger tanks the weight may be more than half a ton. Aquarium stands are sold for most sizes but always consider how much weight your floor will hold.

HOOD AND LIGHT

Most marine tanks which are bought in aquarium stores come with a hood and light fixture. The light is built into the hood so that no metal is exposed to the salt water which otherwise would cause corrosion. The hood is a vital piece of equipment since it prevents fishes from jumping out of the tank and certain animals from climbing out. Octopuses and ribbon eels are notorious for successful escapes, and if you keep these species even the accessory holes must be covered. The hood also keeps salt spray in the tank and foreign matter out. It deters evaporation which generally is considerable, and it retains heat.

Light is important in bringing out the colors of the fishes. It is very beneficial for anemones and live coral, particularly for those species which contain symbiotic algae in their tissues. Algae, which require light for photosynthesis, are needed to provide nourishment for their hosts. The light fixture can be either fluorescent or incandescent. Fluorescent lights burn cooler, do not affect the water temperature greatly, and last longer, making them more economical in the long run. Incandescent lights give off a more natural light, but burn hotter. Again direct sunlight, although it is incomparable for bringing out fish colors, is to be avoided since it cultivates an overabundance of algae.

KIND OF SAND

The type of substrate (sand, gravel, etc.) that you use will determine the effectiveness of your undergravel filter (discussed on the next page), the key element for a healthy aquarium. Limestone, crushed oyster shell, or dolomite should cover the sub-

Dolomite (left) covered with silica sand (right) helps aid good filtration.

sand filter to a depth of 2 to 3 inches (5 to 8 cm.). Limestone is the least preferred. All of these are calcareous materials which act as a buffer to maintain a constant pH, an indicator of the acidity of the water. Since these are coarse materials, they keep sand from clogging the air lift tubes, attached to the undergravel filter.

Cover the limestone, oyster shell, or dolomite with a layer of silica sand about 2 inches (5 cm.) deep. If you collect your own rather than buying from an aquarium store, sterilize it. The sand will be filled with microscopic organisms which may be harmful in the tank. Use a medium grained sand so that it is fine enough to trap large particles of debris on the surface and coarse enough to allow a continuous flow of water through the filter bed. The large particles on the surface can be netted out or siphoned off at cleaning time. Smooth the sand flat so that it forms a layer of constant depth, or else the water will seep into certain areas of the filter bed and be obstructed at others.

SUBSAND FILTER

The subsand or undergravel filter is the most important piece of filtering equipment available and should never be omitted in a salt-water tank. It is inexpensive and requires no maintenance. This filter consists of a sheet of perforated plastic which lies over the entire bottom of the tank beneath the sand. There is a space provided between the filter and the aquarium bottom to allow for water circulation.

Thin plastic tubing joins the air pump outside the aquarium to the air-lifts on the undergravel filter. The compressor pumps air down the tubing while air mixed with water flows back up the air-lift tube. The water moving up the tube is replaced with water from underneath the plastic sheet and gravel. Water flows down through the sand to fill the void below, and in the process the sand grains physically strain out and trap particles of debris.

In addition, vitally important biological filtration is taking place in the sand. Bacteria growing among the sand grains break down the debris collecting there, such as fish excretion, decaying organic matter, and uneaten food. Toxic ammonia is the first by-product of bacterial decomposition, but is converted to less toxic substances by other specialized bacteria. Ammonia build-up is a major problem when a tank is first set up. Refer to "Conditioning Period" in Chapter 4 for a complete explanation.

The effectiveness of the subsand filter depends on the rate of flow of the water, the surface area of the filter bed, the depth of the filtering medium, and the substrate particle size.

A magnet-driven power filter prevents
pollution and will promote the growth
of beneficial bacteria.

OUTSIDE FILTER

An outside filter is a plastic compartment made to hang on
the back of the aquarium. There are two basic types, air-driven
and magnet-driven. Water has to be drawn up by the airlift or
motor-driven pump by siphon into the filter box, and returned.
The filtering unit in each contains two components: activated
carbon (which is more effective than charcoal in salt water) and
filter fiber.

The carbon mechanically strains out particles of debris, but its unique effectiveness is its chemical filtration. Irregularly shaped carbon granules possess a high internal surface area which absorbs organic particles and inorganic ions. This reduces the amount of dissolved organic matter which would be harmful to the fishes if allowed to build up. The carbon also provides much surface area for the growth of beneficial bacteria. Some of the more expensive filters contain ion exchange resins, the main component of which is simply activated carbon. It is presently unknown how long the carbon's usefulness can last, so it is wise to change at least one-half of it every two weeks.

The filter fiber, the second component in the outside filter, mechanically strains particles from the water. The fiber may be spun polyester, wool, sponge, or other similar material, but avoid spun glass since it breaks down in salt water.

The effectiveness of the outside filter depends on the rate of flow of water through the filter and the quality and freshness of the filtering medium. It should be cleaned weekly at first and should be kept in the dark since it is a good breeding ground for algae. Once the tank has become stable for 6 months or more, the filter may only require cleaning once or twice a month. When feeding, try to keep brine shrimp, worms, or other food away from the filter intake tube in order to avoid unnecessary decay.

ULTRAVIOLET LIGHT FOR PURIFICATION

The need for an ultraviolet light for water purification in an aquarium is a controversial subject. The light comes enclosed in a unit which attaches to the return tube of the outside filter. This is the most efficient arrangement since the light appears to work best on filtered water, and this assures that all of the aquarium water will be exposed to the light. ✓

The ultraviolet light has been used in industry for many years, since it decreases the number of free floating viruses and bacteria in the water. The dosage used for aquariums is too low to directly control parasitic protozoans, but it may affect their life cycle. This would decrease the likelihood and spread of disease.

One problem with the light is that since it does not burn out suddenly, there is no way to see its loss of effectiveness. It has been observed by the author that when the UV light loses its efficiency, outbreaks of parasitic infestations appear to be more common and uncontrollable. If the light is used continuously, as it should be, you must replace the unit each year. Try to obtain one with replaceable bulbs even though most of those on the market presently are sealed shut.

Ozone units are not recommended since the dosage cannot be controlled easily, and ozone can be very toxic. Protein skimmers (air strippers) appear to be unnecessary since they duplicate the work of the carbon in the outside filter.

AERATION

Marine fishes require more aeration than fresh-water fishes since they are usually larger and more active. In addition, salt water contains less dissolved oxygen than fresh water. Strong aeration also helps increase water circulation which is vital for healthy fishes and, particularly, certain invertebrates.

Buy a reliable, well constructed, quiet air compressor of either the vibrator or piston type. Vibrator pumps are not as powerful generally, but are quieter. The dependability of your air pump is essential, since a breakdown could cause the loss of the fishes and/or the death of the bacteria needed in the filter bed.

If many air lines are to be run off of one pump, a gang valve may be necessary. You may also insert a valve in the air line that will block any backflow of water caused by a pump failure.

The vibrator type of air pump is sometimes less powerful, but quieter than a piston type pump.

2. The Water Itself

SYNTHETIC VERSUS NATURAL SEA WATER

Synthetic sea water has undergone great improvements in recent years. It has been discovered that trace elements found in natural sea water are necessary for long term maintenance of marine specimens. Previously, these elements had been omitted from the artificial variety of salt water, but now that they are included, fishes are able to thrive in captivity for many years.

There are several advantages to using the synthetic water. It is available to inland aquarists, is already buffered to the correct pH or acidity level, and contains no parasites or algae which are always present in natural water. However, the latter is not only important when first setting up the tank, but also when making partial water changes. Synthetic water has more standardized components than natural sea water which may become diluted from a recent rain, or polluted.

Ageing is not necessary with synthetic water, and there are no buckets to haul around. If a sudden problem arises in the tank, the artificial water usually can be eliminated as the source of the trouble. Of course, the use of synthetic water does not assure a disease-free or algae-free tank, since these problems can enter the water with the food or new fishes.

If you decide to use synthetic water, mix it with any tap water in a plastic bucket or clean garbage pail rather than directly in the aquarium. Follow the package directions carefully and do not use the water until it turns clear. It is best to wait for 24 hours before using it so that the salt dissolves and the chlorine dissipates. You can aerate it to make it dissolve faster, but this is not necessary. Purchase an inexpensive hydrometer to measure the specific gravity which should read between 1.022 and 1.025. Refer to "Salinity" in Chapter 5 for further information.

Synthetic sea salts create a standardized environment. Mix the synthetic and tap water in a plastic bucket rather than directly in the tank.

COLLECTING SEA WATER

Collecting your own natural sea water can be risky. This water will not have the consistent quality of the artificial substitute, but may work well in many cases. Sea water must be obtained offshore in order to avoid pollution, dilution from river or land runoff, and turbidity. It will contain many organisms which may die and foul the water, and it is likely to contain parasites which will bloom in the confines of an aquarium. Algae may also be overabundant.

Do not use metal buckets for transporting the water. Seal the containers tightly and store them in the dark for two to three weeks. During this period the plankton populations will stabilize, and the natural ammonia will be decomposed by bacteria. Finally, aerate the water for 12 hours and then it will be usable.

In a very few areas, it is possible to buy salt water from public aquariums or from pet shops which buy from them. The water is usually filtered, but the quality can vary greatly. This method is better than collecting your own but not as reliable as synthetic sea water.

HEATING THE WATER

Buy a reliable aquarium heater with a thermostatic control, since maintaining a constant water temperature is crucial for

A submersible aquarium heater with thermostatic control keeps tank water at a constant temperature.

healthy fishes. A fluctuating temperature will lower their resistance to disease and may increase the growth of parasites.

The type of heater you select will depend on the depth and capacity of your aquarium. If the tank is very deep, obtain a long heater or there will be a significant temperature gradient between the top layer of water and the bottom. Allow for at least 2 watts per gallon (4 litres) of water to be heated. A cap over the control knob is preferable since it helps keep the controls from being accidentally jarred or water from splashing into the heater.

If the aquarium is in your house, the heater probably will not be on in the daytime. It basically should be a cushion against a drop in temperature at night. Buy a thermometer which can be placed inside the tank.

Temperature is covered on page 33.

SETTING UP AN ISOLATION TANK

The first few weeks in captivity are crucial for marine fishes. Most of them do not survive the trip from the ocean to your local pet shop. Of those that live, many do not adjust to eating aquarium food, others may be badly damaged in transport, and the majority will have a lowered resistance to disease. For these reasons, take great care in your selection of fishes.

Since it is so challenging and time-consuming to obtain a healthy, stable tank, it is wise to take any possible precautions against introducing disease. One excellent method is to set up a 5- or 10-gallon (20- or 40-litre) aquarium with an undergravel filter and an aerator as an isolation tank. Once the main tank(s) is established, all new fish additions should be isolated in the small aquarium for two weeks. Any parasitic infestation will become obvious during this time and can be treated without infecting the main tank. In addition, if the new fish does not eat, alternative food sources can be tried without risking fouling or competition in the main tank.

When disease breaks out in the main aquarium, the infected fish should be removed to the isolation tank and treated there.

3. Setting Up a Successful Aquarium

1. Rinse the tank and all the equipment that will be in contact with the salt water. Never use soap on any part of the aquarium since it is extremely toxic to fishes. Thoroughly rinse the sand by placing small quantities of it in a mixing bowl and gently stirring it under running tap water. It is also convenient to use a plastic bucket and hose. Follow the same procedure for cleaning the dolomite, crushed oyster shell, etc., and rinse until the water runs off clear.

2. Set the undergravel filter in place without letting it touch the sides of the tank. Otherwise, it will show after the substrate is added. Connect the air lines to the air lifts on the filter and then to the air pump. If you have many lines to attach, use a gang valve. If you have a safety valve to keep water from accidentally siphoning back into the pump, insert that also.

3. Spread the rinsed dolomite or crushed oyster shell evenly over the filter. It should be approximately 3 inches (7.5 cm.) deep. Smooth the rinsed sand evenly over the first layer to a depth of 2 inches (5 cm.).

4. Hang the outside filter on the back of the tank. If it contains charcoal or activated carbon, rinse it thoroughly to remove the loose particles. If the filter is air-driven rather than motor-driven, attach the air line to the gang valve.

5. Put the UV sterilizer in place, adding extra tubing if necessary. This unit should be attached to the return line of the outside filter to insure that all water passing through the sterilizer has been filtered for increased efficiency. Be sure that all tubing through which water flows is sealed tightly to its connections. If the tubing is too large, you can wrap electrical tape around the filter return line and attach the tubing over this. If the tubing connection is not secure, water will be pumped out of the filter and the tank onto the floor.

6. Place a mixing bowl in the tank and pour the salt water into the bowl to avoid upsetting the sand. In order to allow room for the coral and/or rocks, fill the tank to several inches below the top. Fill the outside filter with water also.

7. Start up the aerator, filter, and sterilizer, and set the controls on the heater. Adjust the gang valve so that all the air lifts transmit an equal amount of air.

8. It is essential to provide a wide variety of habitat for the fishes and invertebrates. By providing hiding places, the animals will be more at ease in their artificial environment. If there are only one or two good crevices, they will fight continually for them since many fishes are very territorial. Coral is both decorative and functional, but try to buy branching corals as opposed to head corals. The latter accumulate too much debris.

All dead coral should be thoroughly soaked in a separate container in $\frac{1}{4}$ pint ($\frac{1}{8}$ litre) of bleach per gallon (4 litres) of fresh water. Leave it there for 24 hours and then rinse it until no odor of bleach remains. Then soak it in salt water for several days and rinse it. Bleach is highly toxic to marine life so it is best to be overly cautious. If the coral is bought from a pet shop, it probably has been disinfected already.

Stones and rocks may be used only if they lack metallic minerals since these too are toxic to fishes. Sandstone is safe to use. The rocks should be boiled, scrubbed, and rinsed before you place them in the tank.

Coral and rocks tend to collect food particles and algae and, therefore, should be soaked in scalding water during your twice-monthly cleanings. It is usually not necessary to rebleach them. This step may be omitted if you are trying to culture green algae, or if the coral is overgrown with invertebrates.

It is possible to add a piece of coral or rock outside of the back of the tank to give the impression of depth. A piece of blue cloth taped to the back of the aquarium is also very appealing for appearance purposes.

9. Allow the tank to operate for 24 to 48 hours before introducing the fishes. During this time the water temperature can be adjusted.

4. Selecting and Maintaining Fishes

PLANNING AND CHOOSING MARINE FISHES

Whether you intend to collect your own marine life or buy from a shop, you should first plan the type of tank you would like to establish and the type of animals you want to keep. Your aquarium can hold fishes exclusively, invertebrates solely, or a carefully chosen mixture of both. You may wish to own large, aggressive, showy fishes or small, docile, perky ones. A haphazard collection can lead to constant fin-nipping, competition for food, and often death. It is best to start with a few inexpensive fishes since they are generally hardier and more expendable in the learning stage. If you begin with the most expensive, delicate fishes, you may lose them during the critical first two weeks.

The temperament of the animals you choose will affect the mood as well as health and stability of the aquarium. Some of the most beautiful ones (e.g. angelfishes) are highly territorial and aggressive and can evoke constant anxiety from the other fishes. Others, such as the larger damselfishes, are very active and will chase tankmates of any size and often nip their fins or force them to cower among the coral.

Such aggression, if continued, can lead to infected wounds, faded colors, lack of feeding, and eventually death for the victim. Many fishes can be dangerous around invertebrates if not selected properly. Size can be a critical factor in inducing hostility. Two angelfishes of the same size may fight until one or both are killed. On the other hand, a very small fish in a tank with a large one and insufficient cover will very likely end up as a meal. Lionfishes, for example, are notorious for eating their smaller tankmates. In spite of these extremes, some aggression is beneficial for aquarium animals, since it generates exercise as well as water currents.

Many docile fishes such as the surg___, ___ tain wrasses, and butterflyfishes are ve__ colorful and active. Some animals which a___ an aquarium are cleaner wrasses and scav___ wrasses eat parasites from the fishes, and the s___ hermit crabs, eat leftover debris on the bottom of ___.

Unlike fresh-water fishes, it is usually impossible ___ the sex of your marine counterparts. Refer to Chapter ___ mation on sexing certain species. If you intend to try ___ing them, you generally will have to select a matched pair or purchase many individuals of one species.

TANK CAPACITY

Many formulas have been derived for estimating the number of animals you can maintain in an aquarium. The only thing certain is that the tank capacity for marine life is lower than for fresh-water life due to the fishes' demand for more oxygen, cleaner water, and because of their fragile nature. The capacity will depend on the size of the tank, the efficiency of the filters, and whether the fishes or invertebrates are active or inactive. A very general rule would be about one inch ($2\frac{1}{2}$ cm.) of fish for every two gallons ($7\frac{1}{2}$ litres) of water. The aquarium can hold more fishes than this if it is 100 gallons (400 litres) or more. A sample community tank holding 26 gallons (100 litres) of water might contain three clownfishes, an anemone, a cleaner wrasse, a royal gramma, a yellow tang, a mandarin, a jawfish, and a flame scallop.

The safest way to determine the capacity of your tank is to observe over a period of time the behavior and health of the fishes and the cleanliness of the tank. When the fishes start to become overly aggressive, show frayed fins, often become diseased, and the tank seems to need cleaning frequently, you have reached or exceeded the maximum sustainable life.

CONDITIONING PERIOD

It is crucial to understand a little about biological filtration before placing any fishes in the new aquarium. The subsand filter does not function at full capacity for the first two weeks of operation and sometimes it requires up to two months. During this time the filter bed is becoming "conditioned," and the fishes are highly vulnerable to ammonia or nitrite poisoning.

The conditioning process involves several steps. First, hetero-

introduced into the water on the fishes, from
your hands, etc. They break down fish excretion and
organic matter, such as uneaten food. The product is
ammonia which builds up in the first few weeks and can be
highly toxic to marine fishes.

Next, the autotrophic, nitrifying bacteria become established
in the filter bed. They consume ammonia and convert it first to
nitrites and then to the less toxic nitrates. Finally, a third class of
bacteria, the denitrifiers, reduce the nitrites and nitrates to
nitrous oxide or molecular nitrogen (N_2). This continuous cycle
allows bacteria to remove harmful waste products which otherwise would build up to a poisonous level in water.

Since the new fishes are extremely vulnerable to ammonia and
nitrite poisoning during the first month or so, it is critical to start
with hardy specimens. This can be the most challenging or
possibly discouraging time for the aquarist since many fishes can
be lost during this period if it is not handled wisely. The safest
approach but the one requiring the most patience is to start with
several inexpensive damselfishes during the first two weeks. These
fishes are hardy and not as sensitive to ammonia as some and will
supply a continuous source of food for the growing bacteria.

Monitor the nitrite level with a nitrite test kit during the conditioning period. The toxic nitrites will reach a peak and then
decline after about two weeks. If there are too few fishes in the
tank, it may take as much as a month or more to peak out. At
this time it should be safe to remove the damselfishes and put in an
equal or smaller number of the desired specimens. If too many
are put in all at once, the bacteria in the filter bed will not be
able to handle the increased load and the ammonia may again
build up to toxic levels. Add only one new animal a week in
order to allow the nitrifying bacteria to increase and keep pace
with the additional waste products.

It is possible to speed up the conditioning process greatly by
adding sand from an established marine aquarium. The sand
will be laden with bacteria so do not wash it before adding it to
the tank. Use the nitrite test kit to determine when it is safe to
add your animals.

SELECTING HEALTHY FISHES

If you buy your marine fishes rather than collecting them, try
to locate a reliable aquarium supplier. This can be a source of
valuable advice if you are discriminating. A shop's display tanks

When you first set up your tank, a nitrogen test kit will show you when it is safe to introduce new fishes.

should be clean and contain no dead fishes. Avoid specimens with signs of disease such as white spots on the fins or body, clouded eyes, frayed fins, or unnaturally pale colors. If the fish is sluggish, breathing very rapidly, or hovering at the surface, do not buy it. Ask the store clerk to feed the fish if you have any doubts about it, or if it is very expensive. If it does not eat, pass it by. Avoid any fish which brushes its body against the coral as if trying to scratch something off. This is usually the first sign of parasites. Avoid extremely small, young fishes as they can be quite fragile. Although it is difficult to determine the state of health of most invertebrates, anemones should be fully inflated with all their tentacles extended unless they have been fed recently.

Some aquarium suppliers quarantine their fishes for a week before they sell them. This is an excellent procedure since problems such as disease, internal parasites, or failure to feed or adapt to an aquarium will show up during this time. If your pet shop does not do this, set up your own quarantine tank in order to protect the established fishes already in your tank. (See Isolation tank on page 23.)

Healthy Fishes   29

Be certain your aquarium is completely ready before you bring your first fishes home. When transporting the fishes, keep them in the dark and out of direct sunlight or heat. If you have far to travel, have the bag filled at the store with pure oxygen. Float the bag in your aquarium for 15 minutes so that the water temperature in the bag adjusts to that of the tank water. Next, either lift the fish out of the bag with a wet hand or pour the fish into a net lying over a bucket. Immediately place the net and fish in the aquarium. This avoids adding the store water to the tank and possibly contaminating it.

It often is very tricky to introduce a new fish into an established tank, particularly if the old residents are extremely territorial or aggressive. Angelfishes or damselfishes may relentlessly try to drive out an intruder. Even docile clownfishes can become aggressive towards a newcomer. If compatible species have been chosen, however, the problem is minimized. Two possible methods to reduce the conflicts are to feed the old residents as a distraction while the new one is added, or to add the new one while the tank is being cleaned and territories are temporarily disrupted.

FEEDING

Marine fishes as well as fresh-water fishes appear to do better on live food than on the dry variety. Many fishes will not touch anything else. One of the most popular foods has been live brine shrimp. Their nutritional food value, however, is questionable. In addition, they are a potential source of parasites.

Brine shrimp eggs may be purchased in aquarium shops and hatched in 24 to 48 hours in either salt water taken from your tank or in a mixture of 6 tablespoons of table salt to $\frac{3}{4}$ gallon (3 litres) of water. Do not pour the shrimp into the aquarium since the egg shells can kill a fish if eaten. Siphon the hatched brine shrimp into a net and dip the net in the tank. The small brine shrimp may also help tempt a fussy eater to feed.

Tubifex worms have been used successfully for years and do not seem to have any drawbacks. Dry food may be used as a supplement for those that will accept it, but it should not form the bulk of their diet. Pieces of fish or shrimp may also be used as a supplement, but many of the oily types of fish will foul the water very quickly.

Since tangs and butterflyfishes eat algae in the ocean, you can feed them bits of spinach or lettuce if they do not eat worms.

Many hobbyists cultivate rich growths of green algae in the tank for these species.

Since fishes are used to feeding almost continuously in the ocean, it is best to give them several small meals each day rather than one large one. Feed them slowly so that no food is left over to rot. If one fish dominates at feeding time, put in a large amount of food so all animals will have a chance. Another method is to feed the one until its stomach is full and then feed the others.

Anemones need to be fed only once a week and can go for great periods of time without food. Feed them by dropping worms, scallops, or fish on their tentacles.

AQUARIUM MAINTENANCE

In spite of all the filters you can put on your tank, there will still be some build-up of nitrates and a depletion of trace elements in the water. To insure a healthy tank, siphon out $\frac{1}{5}$ of the water in the tank every two weeks. Once the tank has become stable for 6 months or more, the water may need these partial changes only once a month. While removing the water, siphon the detritus and unwanted algae off the surface of the sand. To increase efficiency, use a net to collect large particles of debris off the bottom prior to siphoning. Since most nitrification occurs in the top inch or two of sand, try not to disturb this layer too much when cleaning.

Remove your dead coral, unless it is overgrown with invertebrates, and soak it in scalding tap water to remove trapped debris and excess algae before replacing it. If the coral is a branching type and does not tend to collect particles, this step may not be necessary.

Aquarium shops sell sponges attached to long sticks which can be used to clean the algae off the sides of the tank and improve visibility. Clean the outside filter by rinsing the components in tap water and changing at least one half of the carbon every two weeks. Never use soap for cleaning any part of the aquarium as it is highly toxic even in minute quantities.

Always avoid changing 100 per cent of the aquarium water or disrupting the filter bed even if the tank is being relocated. If it is not possible to transport the water, try to leave the filter bed intact with enough water to cover it. Often aquarists believe that the sand is dirty and should be siphoned out and cleaned every six months or so. This is entirely wrong since a stable, bacteria-laden filter bed is what you have worked so hard to obtain. If it is cleaned, you will have to go through the entire conditioning process again and will be putting your fishes through unnecessary stress. The only time a subsand filter should be disturbed is during cases of extreme parasitic infestations when the whole tank must be sterilized.

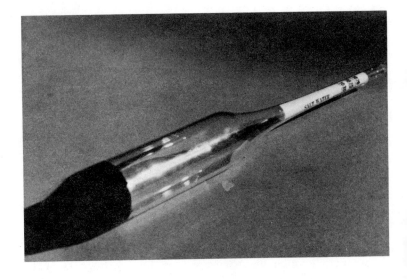

A hydrometer measures the specific gravity of the salt water and enables you to maintain the desired salinity.

5. A Stable Environment

TEMPERATURE

Temperature fluctuation is one of the leading causes of disease and death among captive marine fishes. A rapid temperature change may reduce a fish's resistance to disease by affecting its metabolism. A temperature change may also affect the reproductive rate of parasites since many remain at a dormant level at 23°C (73°F), but will reproduce and grow rapidly at 27°C (80°F). There is often an outbreak of the disease called salt water ich after a large temperature change. To further complicate the problem, the amount of dissolved oxygen in the water is reduced at increased temperatures.

The water temperature range for a tropical marine tank is 21°C (70°F) to 27°C (80°F), with 23°C (73°F) being optimal. Avoid sunny windows, radiators, or drafts and use a heater to stabilize the temperature in the winter and at night.

SALINITY

Purchase a hydrometer to monitor the specific gravity of the salt water. Evaporation from the tank is a constant problem and will increase the salinity. When this occurs, add distilled or "aged" fresh water. Use tap water and hold it in a pail or pan outside the aquarium for several days in order to dissipate the chlorine. If the salt water should become too dilute, simply remove the hood for several days to allow for evaporation.

When reading the hydrometer, wait until it stops bobbing in the water. Turn off the air supply if necessary. The salinity should be 34 parts per thousand, but since the hydrometer measures specific gravity, and is temperature-dependent, it should read 1.024 at 21°C (70°F) and 1.022 at 27°C (80°F). If the hydrometer sits too high in the water, the water is too salty.

pH

The pH of the salt water is a measure of its acidity. The correct range for marine life is from 7.5 to 8.3. The pH is rarely a problem in a tank which has been set up properly, since the

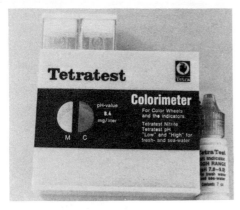

Use an inexpensive pH test kit to test the acidity of the water in the tank.

water is buffered by the dolomite, sand, and coral due to their high calcium content.

If an inexplicable problem arises in the aquarium, the pH should be tested. There are several inexpensive pH test kits available on the market. If the pH is not at the correct level, there may be too many dissolved organics in the water. Check to see that the filter bed is at least 3 inches (7.5 cm.) deep and replace part of the water and carbon. Siphon the detritus from the bottom of the tank and determine whether or not the aquarium is overcrowded.

NITRITES

The nitrites must be monitored, particularly during the conditioning period when the tank is first set up. An inexpensive nitrite test kit will let you know if the nitrification of ammonia to nitrites and nitrates is proceeding properly and will show you when it is safe to introduce new fishes.

The nitrite level should reach a peak in two weeks or more depending on the number of animals present. If the nitrite level does not decrease after a month or so, or if there is ever a second peak, check the tank for dead animals, decaying food, disruption of the filter bed, or a drastic salinity change. Never increase the number of animals in the aquarium or the amount of food quickly since the filter bed will not be able to compensate for such a sudden change.

Never use antibiotics or any drugs that will kill bacteria in the tank. Always use the quarantine tank for treating sick animals, or else the medicine will kill the bacteria in the filter bed and the ammonia level will again rise. It can take months to recondition a tank after antibiotics have been added.

6. Diseases of Marine Fishes

STRESS

Stress in fishes as in humans can trigger disease outbreaks which otherwise might have remained dormant or harmless. A fish is under stress when placed in an artificial environment (i.e., the aquarium), or when the tank's temperature, pH, or salinity fluctuate, when the water is polluted with decaying food, when it is overcrowded, when the fish's diet is inadequate, and when the fish is frightened or injured. A fish in an aquarium reaches a very delicate equilibrium with its environment. If kept in balance, a tank can be maintained for years with little or no loss of life. If the equilibrium is upset, the fish is under stress, its resistance to disease is lowered, and it becomes susceptible to invasion from the ever-present parasites, etc.

Most disease outbreaks and losses of fishes occur when the tank is first set up. It takes from two weeks to six months for the bacteria in the filter bed to reach peak efficiency in breaking down waste products and converting toxic ammonia and nitrites to the less harmful nitrates. A high level of ammonia and nitrites in the aquarium will put the fishes under physiological stress and lower their resistance. In addition, many fishes are under stress when first adjusting to their new environment and tankmates.

PREVENTIVE MEDICINE

In order to reduce loss of life at these critical early stages, follow the instructions in Chapter 4. Try to buy fishes that have been in an aquarium at least one week, and keep them in a quarantine tank at home for two weeks. Do not put them with fishes that you have had for some time until you are sure that they are free of disease. Isolate all abnormal fishes at the first sign of a problem. Never treat a fish in the main tank since many chemicals used to combat disease will kill many of the beneficial organisms in the filter bed. The loss of ammonification and nitrification in the filtering system will cause an increase in ammonia and nitrite to a point which may be more deadly to the fishes than the initial disease.

Keep the tank free of decaying food, sudden temperature change or pH or salinity changes, and overcrowding. Avoid disrupting the filter bed or changing all of the water in the tank at one time. Avoid contact between the salt water and metal or any other toxic substances. Never use soap in cleaning any part of the tank or its contents.

Some hobbyists and most professionals sterilize their fishes to remove parasites before placing them in the aquarium. This procedure is highly risky since the chemicals, if misused, can damage or kill the fishes.

One excellent prophylactic measure, however, is the formalin bath. Robert Dempster, Curator Emeritus of Steinhart Aquarium (San Francisco, California), recommends placing the fishes in 1 cc. concentrated formaldehyde (38 per cent) per gallon (4 litres) of aquarium water for one hour. The fishes should be treated every third day for about 10 days. Since formalin will kill desirable protozoans in your aquarium, always use a bucket or quarantine tank, instead of the main aquarium. Aerate the water vigorously since formalin decreases the oxygen saturation of sea water. If the fish appears over-stressed during this procedure, reduce the formalin concentration but maintain the complete hour of treatment. Formalin is a powerful chemical and must be used at the recommended concentration or lower for the time specified. Wait 3 days before retreatment. Do not overdose. Remember, formalin is mainly used as an embalming fluid! Between baths the fishes may be kept in the quarantine tank with either pure sea water or sea water treated with copper sulphate and citric acid.

While the formalin eradicates flukes and acts as a bactericide, copper sulphate kills external ciliates and flagellates. A copper ion concentration of 0.1 to 0.15 ppm (parts per million) should be continued for 10 days. The length of time is important since the life cycle of many ciliates takes about 10 days. The copper will precipitate and become inactive in alkaline water, such as sea water. Consequently a copper test should be done every 24 hours to maintain the appropriate concentration. Inexpensive copper test kits are available in aquarium shops, as is copper sulphate sequestered with citric acid to decrease precipitation.

If you want to mix your own stock solution, dissolve 2.23 grams of copper sulphate ($CuSO_4 \cdot 5H_2O$) and 1.50 grams of citric acid in one litre (33.8 liquid ounces) of distilled or de-ionized water. Add this solution to the aquarium at the rate of 1 cc. per gallon of aquarium water. This will provide a copper concentration of 0.15 $\pm$ 0.03 ppm in the tank. Be sure all measurements, including the volume of the tank, are done accurately.

Use the following formula to determine how much stock solution to add to the tank if the copper test indicates a low copper concentration due to precipitation.

$$\frac{P_1 \times V}{P_2} = S$$

P_1 = required ppm increase in copper concentration
P_2 = desired concentration
V = volume of the tank in gallons
S = cc. of stock solution required to increase the copper concentration to the desired level.

If you do not use this method, add a small amount of the copper sulphate solution at a time until the copper test shows that the correct concentration has been reached.

Never treat invertebrates with copper since they are highly sensitive to it!

SYMPTOMS OF DISEASE

Symptoms indicating a fish is diseased are:
(1) a fish's scraping or brushing against coral, rocks, etc.
(2) spastic uncontrolled movement
(3) lack of appetite
(4) listlessness
(5) unnaturally hovering at the surface or in a dark corner
(6) abnormally pale or darkened color
(7) increased rate of breathing
(8) white spots, growths, and wounds on the fins or body.

PARASITES

Aquarium fishes are continually threatened by parasites which are almost always present on fishes, in sea water, or on their food. When the environmental equilibrium is upset, chronic infections may flare up or new ones arise. In the ocean the fishes can escape from a highly infected area, whereas when they are confined in the aquarium, diseases are transmitted readily, and parasites thrive.

In a stable tank a fish may live with mildly infectious parasites without being adversely affected by them. A healthy fish will often build up an immunity to parasites. However, when the environment becomes unstable through temperature changes, overcrowding, etc., the fish's resistance breaks down and the parasites become severely infectious. An excellent preventive measure is to keep a cleaner wrasse, *Labroides dimidiatus*, in your marine aquarium. These hardy fishes pick parasites from the gills, mouth, and body surface of other fishes.

PROTOZOANS

Cryptocaryon irritans

"White spot disease" or "salt water ich" is the marine counterpart to the fresh-water *Ichthyophthirius*. This disease is caused by a common parasitic ciliate. The surface of the fish, parasitized by *C. irritans*, is covered by small white or grayish vesicles, which are nests created in the skin and gills by the mature parasite. There are three stages in the life cycle of this ciliate. In the first stage it is parasitic and forms the white spots on the fish. In the second, it drops off the fish in order to reproduce, and encysts on the bottom of the tank. This stage takes up to 20 hours to be reached at room temperature. Within the cyst, as many as 200 or more free-swimming ciliates are produced. After about 8 days the third stage ciliates emerge and have 24 hours to find a host. When the host is found, they burrow into the skin and gills and when mature, produce the white spots. The parasites feed on the fish's cells and damage the gill filaments causing severe respiratory problems. Skin lesions may appear, and secondary bacterial infections may kill the fish. Generally, however, the ciliates are the cause of death in heavily infected fishes.

Cause: This disease is rarely encountered in the ocean and appears to be due to the crowded conditions of the aquarium. The development of this parasite is greatest at temperatures of $20°$ to $25°C$ ($68°$ to $77°F$). This infection may stabilize at a low level but will flare up with environmental changes.

Treatment: Ultraviolet irradiation may help to control the *Cryptocaryon's* free-swimming stage, but this has not been proven yet. It does not seem to affect the parasitic first stage.

Copper sulphate, which can be purchased in aquarium shops, is usually the recommended treatment. Unfortunately, it primarily kills only the free-swimming stages of *C. irritans* allowing the parasitic first stage form to continue the life cycle. Formalin, on the other hand, is reported to destroy this first stage. Therefore, the latest cure for this disease requires short formalin baths (see page 36) and prolonged copper sulphate-citric acid treatments (see page 37). Between baths the fishes can be kept in a quarantine tank in sea water treated with copper sulphate. Use a copper test kit daily to maintain the recommended copper concentration. Refer to Preventive Medicine (page 35) for detailed directions.

Since *C. irritans* is highly contagious, remove every fish from the infected tank to the quarantine tank for treatment. Keep all fishes out of the infected aquarium for 10 to 14 days so the parasites in the tank will die due to lack of a host.

Sodium chlorite has been recently tested and found effective against *C. irritans*. Dissolve 126.8 grams of sodium chlorite (80 per cent) in a litre (quart) of water, add enough sodium carbonate to raise the pH to 9, and add 1 cc. of this solution per gallon (4 litres) of aquarium water to the tank. The chlorite concentration will be about 20 ppm. Maintain this level by periodically adding more solution for two weeks in order to eradicate the disease. Do not use an ultraviolet light during this treatment since it may oxidize chlorite to become chlorate, which is highly toxic.

Oodinium ocellatum

"Gill disease" is caused by a dinoflagellate protozoan, *Oodinium ocellatum*. This common parasitic disease can reach epidemic proportions quickly. The parasite attaches to the fish's gills with root-like appendages and drains nourishment from its host. It then drops off, divides, and forms 256 free-swimming flagellated dinospores. Later the dinospores settle to the bottom where they develop into the infective form of dinoflagellates. It takes 7 days at 24°C (75°F) to reach this free-swimming stage, and then the dinoflagellates have 24 hours to find a host or they die.

Symptoms: The fishes will show difficulty in breathing and will hover in a corner of the tank near the surface gasping for air. The parasites become so abundant on the gill filaments that they greatly interfere with respiration. The fish dies of suffocation if not treated immediately. This disease can kill within a few days.

Cause: The rate of progression of the life cycle is dependent on the tank temperature. Under 10°C (50°F) no dinospores are formed. At around 25°C (77°F) the growth rate is optimal. Some fishes develop a temporary resistance to *Oodinium* but become infected when water quality declines, nutrition is poor, or overcrowding exists. Since almost all marine fishes are subject to infection by *Oodinium*, it is vital to maintain high environmental quality in your tank and adequate nutrition.

Treatment: Ultraviolet irradiation may control the free-swimming stages, but this has not been proven yet. Copper sulphate is the recommended treatment. Follow the instructions concerning copper sulphate given for *Cryptocaryon* (page 38).

BACTERIAL INFECTIONS

Vibrio

Vibrio disease, also known as "fin rot," is a common problem in aquariums and also in fish farming. It is caused by the bacteria called *Vibrio*, and can only be diagnosed with laboratory cultures.

Symptoms: The infected fish shows loss of appetite, sluggishness, and skin discoloration. The fins deteriorate, and the body then hemorrhages, with red blotches forming under the scales. The anus may become reddened and inflamed, and internally there is hemorrhaging of the liver, spleen, and kidneys.

Cause: Vibrio is directly affected by environmental conditions, particularly rapid temperature changes. It is a common problem at higher than recommended temperatures. A flare-up of *Vibrio* may also be due to any other factors that lower a fish's resistance to disease. This would include water pollution, increased salinity, overcrowding, bad nutrition, rough handling, and stress.

Treatment: Lesions on the fins and body can be swabbed with aqueous Mercurochrome, potassium permanganate, or acriflavin. Antibiotics such as aureomycin, terramycin, and chloromycetin can be used sparingly and only in an isolation tank, since they do not kill bacteria selectively.

TUBERCULOSIS

Tuberculosis is a common bacterial infection in aquarium fishes. The muscle and subcutaneous tissue may become ulcerated, bones are destroyed, the skin takes on a yellowish tinge, and the muscles become soft. Internally there may be gray-white necrotic areas on the liver, spleen, ovaries, and other organs. With time, the small protuberances grow and coalesce, gradually destroying the healthy tissue. Eventually the larger tumors completely block the circulation of the diseased organs and the fish dies.

Symptoms: Externally infected fishes show loss of appetite and weight. They become listless and hide in dark areas of the tank. Sometimes round gray-black nodules or lesions appear on the skin surface. There may be excessive mucus, the fins may become frayed, and even the bones may become deformed. Since the symptoms of tuberculosis very closely resemble those of some other bacterial diseases, exact diagnosis is impossible without a laboratory culture.

Cause: This chronic disease may be transmitted through infected food or may directly enter open wounds on the body surface.

Treatment: By the time external evidence of the disease appears, much internal damage has already occurred. Little is known about prevention and treatment of tuberculosis. Ultraviolet irradiation may control the level of bacteria in the water but will have no effect on the infected fish. Diseased fishes should be isolated, and dead fishes must be removed immediately to prevent transfer of the disease to other healthy fishes in the same environment.

VIRAL INFECTIONS

Lymphocystis

Lymphocystis is the most common viral disease among aquarium fishes. The virus causes an increase in the growth of cells on the body surface. These cells eventually burst and the skin heals. The disease generally is not fatal, but often is accompanied by a secondary bacterial infection which can be fatal.

Symptoms: The enlarged cells appear as white "tapioca-like" clumps on the skin surface, giving the infection the name "cauliflower disease."

Cause: A fish may become infected by consuming diseased flesh or by coming in contact with the contents of infected cells that have burst. The disease is more common during summer. Fishes with a lowered resistance due to high temperatures, overcrowding, or bad water quality, etc. are most susceptible.

Treatment: Lymphocystis is highly resistant and contagious. There are no known drugs effective against it. Remove the infected fish to an isolation tank and pull or cut off the enlarged cysts. Swab the wound with Mercurochrome, a 1 per cent solution of malachite green, or acriflavin, to prevent fungal infection. Maintain a stable environment for your fishes so they can build up a resistance to the secondary bacterial infection.

FUNGUS

Ichthyophonus hoferi

This is the most common fungus disease to infect aquarium fishes. It can attack any of the internal organs as well as the external surface and obtains nourishment by digesting the living tissue on which it is growing. It generally reproduces asexually by forming spores which enter the host's bloodstream and infect the fish's organs.

Symptoms: Although the fish may appear hungry, it loses weight rapidly and usually dies within several months. It may lose color, show some fin deterioration, and swim erratically due to loss of equilibrium. The skin surface may be covered with yellowish spots.

Cause: A fish becomes infected by consuming fungal spores or the flesh of a contaminated fish.

Treatment: There is no known cure for this infection, but the fish may be dipped in a 1 per cent solution of malachite green for 60 seconds to slow the disease's progression. The infected fish should then be placed in an isolation tank.

PARASITIC WORMS

Benedenia melleni

Benedenia is a common monogenetic trematode or flatworm which attaches to the fish's eyes, nasal cavities, gills, and skin. Adults grow to 5 mm. in length and are almost transparent. Their eggs are laid directly on the fish, and take up to 8 days to hatch. The larvae then have 24 hours to find a host or die. Those that live will mature in 18 days at 22°–26°C (72°–79°F).

Symptoms: The large gray-white triangular parasites may be seen on the fish's body or on the eyes, which become filmed over and burst. A secondary bacterial infection often occurs simultaneously. The fish may attempt to brush against coral or the sides and bottom of the tank.

Cause: Fishes are commonly infested with trematodes (flatworms or flukes), nematodes (roundworms), and cestodes (tapeworms). A fish may not be hurt directly by these parasites unless it is weakened by stress, etc.

Treatment: The safest treatment is to place the infested fish in an aerated bucket of *fresh* water for about 15 minutes to force the parasites to drop off. The length of time which is safe varies with each species. Remove the fish if it shows signs of distress.

Often this does not eradicate every worm, so stronger measures may be necessary. The formalin bath described on page 36 is an excellent treatment. Place the infested fish in a heavily aerated bucket or quarantine tank treated with 1 cc. concentrated (38 per cent) formaldehyde per gallon (4 litres) of sea water for one hour. Repeat this treatment three times (once every three days) in order to kill the eggs.

The cleaner wrasse, *Labroides dimidiatus*, and other cleaner fishes feed on ectoparasites inhabiting the skin, gills, and mouths of fishes. That is why one of these hardy fishes should be kept in the aquarium at all times.

PARASITIC CRUSTACEANS

Argulus

Fish lice of the genus *Argulus* are large external parasites which sometimes infest seahorses. These brown copepods reach several millimetres in length, attach to the skin surface, and inject a venom which can kill small fishes. In larger fishes this can cause cell degeneration and open wounds which are subject to secondary bacterial infection.

Symptoms: The large brown copepods are visible running over the surface of the host.

Treatment: Argulus is too hardy to be treated with drugs or chemicals. Remove the parasites with tweezers or place a drop of alcohol on them. If they have gained control of the tank, it will have to be sterilized along with all the aquarium utensils. Raw wounds on the fishes should be swabbed with acriflavin or aqueous Mercurochrome.

GAS BUBBLE DISEASE

This non-infectious problem occurs when the fish's system becomes supersaturated with oxygen or nitrogen. Air bubbles form in the circulatory system, the surface of the skin, inside the mouth, and in the body cavity. Great tissue damage can occur.

Symptoms: Air bubbles are visible under the skin surface and fins. Respiration may be difficult.

Cause: This problem may occur if air is bubbled under pressure through an air stone at high temperatures such as 28° to 29°C (82° to 85°F). It may also occur if there is a leak in the intake side of a power filter causing air to be forced back into the aquarium.

Treatment: The fishes will recover if placed in fresh sea water.

If the above problems are corrected, the gases built up in the water will dissipate naturally.

POPEYE

Symptoms: The fish's eye appears to be protruding from its socket and eventually may burst and cause death.

Cause: There are many theories about the cause of "popeye" or *exophthalmus*. It is a common occurrence in captive fishes and can be due to: (1) a build-up of fluids supersaturated with gases as in gas bubble disease; (2) a bacterial infection; (3) trematode or flatworm larvae in the eye; (4) kidney infection; (5) drug overdose; (6) injury from rough handling.

Treatment: Many times this disease will disappear very rapidly without any treatment at all. Do not attempt to puncture the eye to relieve the pressure. It may be treated with a 1 per cent solution of silver nitrate followed by a 1 per cent solution of potassium dichromate if it is thought to be caused by trematodes. Check for trouble which might be causing gas bubble disease.

If you handle many fishes and find popeye to be a major problem, it may be due to net injuries. Professionals use the tranquilizer, quinaldine, before moving fishes to reduce this problem. The exact dosage must be used, however, or you will kill your specimens.

Make a 10 per cent stock solution of quinaldine and add 0.4 cc. of this solution for each gallon (4 litres) of sea water. Small fishes should be left in the solution for only 30 seconds to 2 minutes. Larger specimens, such as large groupers, may require 5 minutes. Never leave the fishes in the tranquilizer for more than 10 minutes. Quinaldine can be purchased from any large chemical supply house.

TANK STERILIZATION

If sterilization is required, you should review your entire method of aquarium maintenance. If the recommendations in the first five chapters of this book are followed, tank sterilization should rarely if ever be necessary. It is used only as a last resort when all else fails since it means starting from scratch in reconditioning the filter bed.

If conditions deteriorate to this level, it indicates that diseased fishes passed through quarantine, healthy specimens were fed contaminated food, or most likely that the aquarium environment had not reached a stable equilibrium.

A long-handled cleaning brush will remove algae from your tank's sides.
Remember: don't use soap!

When the tank becomes stabilized over a period of many months, the fishes build up a strong resistance to parasite invasions, bacterial and fungal infections, etc. and wounds heal faster. Examine the following questions to determine the source of imbalance.

(1) Are the nitrite level, ammonia level, temperature, pH, and salinity constant and within a normal range?

(2) Is there enough sand covering the undergravel filter to insure its efficiency?

(3) Were too many fishes added before the filter bed could handle their wastes?

(4) Is the outside filter effective?

(5) Is the water added during the partial water changes contaminated?

(6) Is there overcrowding?

(7) Is there decaying food in the tank?

(8) Are there excessive algal blooms?

Sterilize all equipment by placing the utensils in the aquarium and filling it with about $\frac{1}{2}$ ounce (15 millilitres) of liquid chlorine bleach per gallon (4 litres) of fresh water. Let everything soak for several days, rinse thoroughly, and dry completely. Be sure there is no trace or smell of chlorine remaining, since it is highly toxic to fishes.

Parts of a Fish

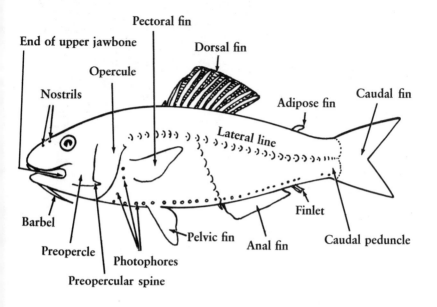

End of upper jawbone

Nostrils

Opercule

Pectoral fin

Dorsal fin

Adipose fin

Caudal fin

Lateral line

Barbel

Preopercle

Preopercular spine

Photophores

Pelvic fin

Anal fin

Finlet

Caudal peduncle

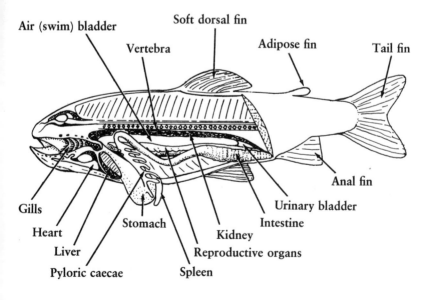

Air (swim) bladder

Vertebra

Soft dorsal fin

Adipose fin

Tail fin

Anal fin

Urinary bladder

Intestine

Kidney

Reproductive organs

Spleen

Stomach

Pyloric caecae

Liver

Heart

Gills

Use an aquarium net to
transfer your fish safely
from one tank to another.

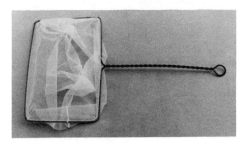

INCOMPATIBILITY CHART

FISHES	INCOMPATIBLE WITH
Angelfishes	Some angelfishes, crustaceans, sponges, coral
Butterflyfishes	Coral, small invertebrates
Surgeonfishes	Sponges, coral, crustaceans
Moorish idols	Some Moorish idols
Anemonefishes	Groupers, triggerfishes
Damselfishes	Some damselfishes, groupers, triggerfishes
Wrasses	Groupers, crabs, sea urchins, small invertebrates
Lionfishes	Most small fishes, damselfishes, gobies, wrasses, anemonefishes
Triggerfishes	Most fishes, triggerfishes, gobies, filefishes, damselfishes, anemonefishes, sea urchins, shellfishes, coral, crustaceans
Filefishes	Triggerfishes, coral, sponges, small crustaceans
Puffers	Other puffers, small crustaceans, molluscs
Trunkfishes	Triggerfishes, groupers, sponges, small crabs, small shrimp
Porcupinefishes	Molluscs, sea urchins, crabs, porcupinefishes
Squirrelfishes	Some smaller fishes
Cardinalfishes	Some smaller fishes, occasionally larger fishes
Dragonets or Mandarin fishes	Males incompatible with males
Gobies	Triggerfishes, groupers
Batfishes	Other batfishes
Spadefishes	Sponges, molluscs, crustaceans
Groupers	Some groupers, gobies, damselfishes, anemonefishes, small crustaceans
Basslets	Groupers, triggerfishes
Grunts	Small fishes, molluscs, small crustaceans
Sweetlips	Triggerfishes
Hawkfishes	Some hawkfishes, small fishes, small invertebrates
Scats	None
Jawfishes	Most other fishes
Coral catfishes	None
Seahorses	Groupers, triggerfishes
Pipefishes	Groupers, triggerfishes
Moray eels	Small fishes, crustaceans

7. Suitable Species for Your Aquarium

ANGELFISHES—Family Chaetodontidae

The showy, domineering angelfishes are the royalty of the aquarium world. As they glide majestically through the water, they command a position at the top of the pecking order. While they belong to the same family as the butterflyfishes, they are distinguished by possessing sharp pre-opercular spines. Their bodies are laterally compressed and display vivid designs which change dramatically as the fishes grow. Many juveniles have markings and coloration entirely different from their adult counterparts.

Angelfishes have small mouths and small teeth but a voracious appetite. Since their natural diet consists of coral, sponges, worms, algae, and crustaceans, never include them with invertebrates. In an aquarium these fishes will thrive on *Tubifex* worms, brine shrimp, and lettuce or green algae.

Since they are highly territorial, they require at least a 25-gallon (100-litre) tank and much cover. In order to reduce aggression, avoid putting two angelfishes of the same species in the same tank unless they differ in size by several inches or are a mated pair. Angelfishes of different species will coexist all right; however, they require a large tank since they grow to one to two feet (30 to 60 cm.) long. If properly cared for, most of these fishes are fairly hardy and will eat readily.

NOTE: Within each family, the species are arranged alphabetically by scientific name. A parenthesis around a biologist's name indicates that he is credited as author of the species but named a different genus than is accepted today.

Lemon Peel   *Centropyge flavissimus* Cuvier

As the name suggests, the body of this species is brilliant yellow. The eye is ringed in blue and the gill cover bears a blue vertical edge. Juvenile lemon peels are similar in coloration to the rock beauty, *Holacanthus tricolor*. The caudal fin and the anterior part of the body are bright yellow while the posterior half is dark blue.

This species is found in the South Pacific including Hawaii and grows to 4 inches (10 cm.). The lemon peel can be fed brine shrimp, worms, or dried flake food.

Flame Angelfish *Centropyge loriculus*
This fish has only recently been imported into the continental United States. It is bright red with irregular dark vertical bars, grows to 5 inches (12.5 cm.), and is found in the waters around the Hawaiian Islands.

Potter's Angelfish *Centropyge potteri* Jordan and Metz *
This small angelfish grows to about 4 inches (10 cm.) in length and has a good temperament when mixing with other fishes. Its body is rust colored with wavy, vertical blue barring, and the caudal fin is dark blue. This species is found in the shallow waters of the tropical Indo-Pacific including Hawaii.

Queen Angelfish *Holacanthus ciliaris* Linnaeus **
The body of this elegant fish varies from blue to yellow with a distinctive black spot ringed and speckled with blue on the forehead. The posterior edge of the gill cover is brilliant blue as are the edges of the dorsal and anal fins. Its pectoral, pelvic, and caudal fins are orange-yellow at all stages of developement.

Young of this species have three light blue, narrow curved bars on a dark blue-yellow body. A dark band with two light blue margins passes through the eyes.

The queen angelfish grows to 18 inches to 2 feet (45–60 cm.) and is found from the Bahamas to Brazil as well as the Gulf Coast of Florida and the southern Gulf of Mexico. This species can become aggressive but generally feeds well and is hardy in a stable aquarium.

Blue Angelfish *Holacanthus isabelita* Jordan and Ritter
The basic difference between *Holacanthus isabelita* and *Holacanthus ciliaris* is color variation. The body of the blue angelfish is yellowish or purplish brown while the throat and forehead are dark blue. Most noticeable, however, is the absence of a distinct crown on adult blues. The dorsal and anal fins have

---

*Asterisk indicates this species is illustrated in the full-color photographic section of this book.

blue margins but are yellow posteriorly on blue angelfishes and blue posteriorly on queen angelfishes. The blue's caudal fin has only a yellow posterior edge while the queen's tail fin is solid yellow.

H. isabelita grows to 18 inches (40 cm.) and has been observed in the Gulf of Mexico, off of southern Florida, the Bahamas, and Bermuda. *Holacanthus bermudensis* and *Holacanthus townsendi* were once thought to be separate species but are now considered to be hybrids between the queen and the blue angelfishes. The blue angelfish is often aggressive in an aquarium.

Rock Beauty *Holacanthus tricolor* Bloch *

Juveniles of this species are yellow with a black spot rimmed with blue on the dorsal portion of the body. This ocellus or eyespot grows as the fish matures until eventually the blue is lost, and most of the posterior half of the body becomes black. The anterior portion of the body is bright yellow. So are all the fins, but the dorsal and anal fins are fringed with red. The rock beauty's eyes are edged with blue in both juvenile and adult specimens. It grows to over one foot (30 cm.) in length and has been observed from Georgia to Brazil and off Bermuda and the Bahamas.

Gray Angelfish *Pomacanthus arcuatus* Linnaeus *

Juveniles of this angelfish are black with four light yellow vertical bars which disappear with age. The adults turn gray and have a dark gray-brown spot in the center of each scale. The dorsal and anal fins are elongated into filaments. Pectoral and pelvic fins are dark brown, and the caudal fin has a whitish border. This species grows to 2 feet (60 cm.) and is found from New England to Brazil and also in the Gulf of Mexico.

French Angelfish *Pomacanthus paru* Bloch *

Juvenile French angelfishes are similar to imperial angelfishes *(Pomacanthus imperator)* and gray angelfishes *(Pomacanthus arcuatus)*. The bodies of the young French and gray angelfishes are black with four yellow vertical bars, but these bars are brighter on the French angelfish. The juvenile imperial angelfish can be distinguished by the white bars on its body. The tail fin margin of the gray angelfish is truncated and transparent while that of the French angelfish is curved and yellow.

The adult French angelfish is gray or black with a yellow dorsal filament and scales edged in yellow. This fish is somewhat smaller than the gray angelfish and reaches about 15 inches

Koran Angelfish

(37.5 cm.) in length. It is found from the West Indies to the Florida Keys and has been seen as far north as Massachusetts. Fairly compatible with other fishes, it is very hardy.

Koran Angelfish *Pomacanthus semicirculatus* (Cuvier and Valenciennes)

This is another species which varies greatly from juvenile to adult. The young fishes exhibit alternating thin and thick semi-circular white bands on a blue-black body. The anterior stripes are nearly vertical while the posterior ones curve backwards. These lines are lost with age until the adult fish becomes yellowish anteriorly and gray posteriorly with black or blue spots dotting its sides.

The common name is derived from the Arabic-looking characters on the tail fin of very young fishes. This species ranges from East Africa to Ceylon and the Philippines and grows to 15 inches (37.5 cm.). It is a hardy fish which feeds well.

BUTTERFLYFISHES—Family Chaetodontidae

Butterflyfishes can be an excellent addition to a marine aquarium because of their docile nature and delicate coloration. These fishes have small, laterally compressed bodies with high-set backs and generally are between 3 and 4 inches (7.5 and 10 cm.) long. The colors are often yellows and browns and may vary among six or seven shades for one species. Two distinctive characteristics of most butterflyfishes are the dark eyespots near the tailfin and a dark vertical band passing through the eyes.

While the angelfishes are aggressive, the butterflyfishes are gentle and dainty. They are selective about their food and use their elongated mouths to pick at coral polyps or to reach tiny invertebrates in the coral crevices. In an aquarium, most butterflyfishes require live food. It is sometimes difficult to get them to start feeding in captivity, but most will relish live brine shrimp, worms, and green algae if available. Some of the smaller specimens may require newly hatched brine shrimp, but it is best to avoid such young fishes.

Newly introduced butterflyfishes can be prone to shock. Before placing them in the tank, turn off as many lights as possible and keep the tank light off until the next day. Feed the other members of the aquarium before adding the new fish.

If a butterflyfish is threatened, it will defend itself by erecting its dorsal spines and lowering its head. With its fins extended, it then darts back and forth towards its aggressor. This is a threat display and rarely injures the other fish. Butterflyfishes generally have an excellent temperament for an aquarium and can do well when provided with the proper food.

Foureye Butterflyfish *Chaetodon capistratus* Linnaeus*

This fish ranges from Massachusetts to the Caribbean and the Gulf of Mexico. The name originates from the large black eyespot ringed in white near the caudal fin. The pale gray-yellow body bears many fine dark lines running diagonally from the dorsal and anal fins to the mid-region. A black band edged in yellow passes through the eye. The young display two eyespots and two broad bands on the body.

This species grows to 6 inches (15 cm.) in length and is a fairly hardy aquarium specimen.

Sunburst Butterflyfish *Chaetodon kleini* Bloch

This butterflyfish ranges from East Africa to Indonesia and is golden with a dark band passing through the eyes to the pelvic fins. There may also be a pale reddish band from the dorsal fin to the pelvic fins. Each scale on the posterior portion of the body carries a dark spot.

This is generally a hardy fish which feeds well and grows to 5 inches (12.5 cm.).

Raccoon Butterflyfish *Chaetodon lunula* Lacépède *

The raccoon butterflyfish is found from the Red Sea through Malaysia and Indonesia to the Hawaiian Islands. Its body is yellowish with a wide black band through the eyes followed by a white bar. A dark triangular area runs from behind the gill cover up to the spiny dorsal fin. A dark stripe made up of spots follows each row of scales on the body. The base of the soft dorsal is outlined by a dark line which merges into a circle on the caudal peduncle.

This fish can attain 8 inches (20 cm.) in length and is imported frequently.

Black-Backed Butterflyfish *Chaetodon melannotus* Bloch and Schneider *

This butterflyfish has a yellowish-silver body with a narrow black band through the eyes. There are many dark oblique lines running up to the dorsal fin along the body's scale rows, with a large black spot on the caudal peduncle.

This fish is found throughout the Indo-Pacific and the Red Sea and grows to 7 inches (17.5 cm.).

---

*Asterisk indicates this species is illustrated in the full-color photographic section of this book.

Lemon Butterflyfish *Chaetodon miliaris* Quoy and Gaimard

The body is silvery and yellow, speckled with small dark spots which form vertical rows. It has a black vertical bar through the eye and one on the caudal peduncle. This hardy species grows to 5 inches (12.5 cm.) and is common around the Hawaiian Islands.

Common Butterflyfish *Chaetodon ocellatus* Bloch

This species is also known as the spotfin butterflyfish due to a large dark spot at the base of the dorsal fin. The top of the soft dorsal also bears a small black mark. The body is white with a black stripe running through the eye. All of the fins are a brilliant yellow except the pectoral fins which are translucent.

These fishes grow to 8 inches (20 cm.) and are found from New England to Brazil and in the Gulf of Mexico.

Banded Butterflyfish *Chaetodon striatus* Linnaeus *

The body of this fish displays four black bars on a white background. It is distinguished by having the snout, top of the head, and the caudal peduncle tinged in yellow. Narrow gray lines outline the diagonal scale rows. The pelvic fins are black except for the spines which are white. The young have a small black spot on the dorsal fin.

This species grows to 6 inches (15 cm.) and is found on both sides of the Atlantic. On the American side, it ranges from New Jersey to Brazil and the Gulf of Mexico.

Tear Drop Butterflyfish *Chaetodon unimaculatus* Bloch *

The body is yellowish with a tear drop-shaped black spot on the side. Through the eyes is a vertical black band and another appears from the soft dorsal through the caudal peduncle to the anal fin. This hardy fish is fairly common in the tropical Indo-Pacific and grows to 7 inches (17.5 cm.).

Vagabond Butterflyfish *Chaetodon vagabundus* Linnaeus *

This butterflyfish is commonly found off the east coast of Africa and in the Indo-Pacific. Its body is yellow to gray with a black stripe through the eye and a black outline from the dorsal fin to the caudal peduncle and anal fin. Its sides display diagonal stripes running obliquely upwards to the dorsal fin and downwards to the anal fin. The tail fin bears a black band and edge. The young have a large black spot on the soft dorsal.

Diagonal Butterflyfish

The vagabond butterflyfish grows to 6 inches (15 cm.) and is fairly hardy in an aquarium.

Copperbanded Butterflyfish *Chelmon rostratus* (Linnaeus) *
This is one of the most colorful representatives of the butterflyfishes. The body is silver with five brilliant copper-colored vertical bands. A black eyespot adorns the soft dorsal and a black bar appears on the caudal peduncle. The jaws are somewhat elongated and are used to reach into coral crevices for food.
This species originates in the tropical Indo-Pacific and grows to 8 inches (20 cm.). Although it can be a fussy eater, it does well once started and thrives on a continued supply of live brine shrimp or small worms.

Longnosed Butterflyfish *Forcipiger flavissimus* Jordan and McGregor *
This species feeds more readily than the copperbanded and has a very elongated snout. Its body is a brilliant yellow shaded with orange while the head is black dorsally and white ventrally.

A black spot is located beneath the caudal peduncle. The dorsal spines are very long and are used as a defense mechanism.

This fish can be aggressive, particularly towards members of its own species. Found along coral reefs and rocky coasts from East Africa to the west coast of North America, it is fairly common near the Hawaiian Islands. It can attain a length of 9 inches (22.5 cm.).

Banner Fish *Heniochus acuminatus* Linnaeus *
This butterflyfish is distinguished from the others by the high, arched back and the long banner-like dorsal fin. Its body is silver with two black stripes, and although it greatly resembles the beautiful Moorish idol, there is no relationship. The soft dorsal fin and the caudal fin are yellow.

The banner fish ranges from East Africa through the central Pacific and is a very hardy, lively fish. It eats well, even taking dry food, and is compatible with other fishes. It does well as a small aquarium specimen but can grow very large—to 10 inches (25 cm.).

SURGEONFISHES OR TANGS—
Family Acanthuridae

This group of fishes derives its name from the sharp spines on the sides of the caudal peduncle. In the yellow tang, *Zebrasoma flavescens,* the spine is movable and folds back into a groove. In the genus *Naso* the spines are immovable. The dorsal, anal, and pelvic spines are poisonous in many larval and some adult species of *Naso.* All surgeonfishes should be handled with care since they are capable of inflicting serious wounds.

The surgeonfish's oval-shaped body is laterally compressed and covered with tiny scales. The mouth is small and contains teeth specialized for grazing on filamentous algae. In the aquarium surgeonfishes should be offered spinach or lettuce if green algae is not available. Some Indo-Pacific species feed on zooplankton, and most captive specimens adapt to consuming brine shrimp and worms.

The coloration of each species of surgeonfish can vary greatly depending on their mood, the amount of light falling on them, or their geographical location. For example, the yellow tang

Philippine Surgeonfish

is a brilliant yellow around Hawaii and is brown in the Indo-Pacific. It is whitish when sleeping and displays a white streak on its side when frightened. The blue tang, *Acanthurus coeruleus*, is yellow as a juvenile and blue as an adult.

Occasionally surgeonfishes can be hard to keep since they are prone to disease. Highly sensitive to temperature changes, they go into shock easily. Most members of this family do best if the water does not fall below 26°C (80°F). The yellow tang appears to be one of the hardiest members of this group and is not severely affected by slight temperature variations.

There are 17 genera and about 100 species of surgeonfishes found mainly among the coral reefs of tropical seas. All of these fishes can grow very large, but most are under 20 inches (50 cm.) in length. Some are said to be good eating, while in other regions they are considered poisonous due to their diet of toxic algae.

Achilles Tang *Acanthurus achilles* Shaw *

Although the Achilles tang is imported fairly frequently, it is a delicate fish and is prone to disease. The body is a rich brown with a brilliant, eliptical orange area surrounding the spine on

---

*Asterisk indicates this species is illustrated in the full-color photographic section of this book.

the caudal peduncle. The base of the dorsal and anal fins and half of the caudal fin are also orange.

This elegant fish is found in the inshore turbulent waters along the China coast, around Polynesia and the Hawaiian Islands. It grows to 10 inches (25 cm.) in length.

Doctorfish *Acanthurus chirurgus* Bloch

The doctorfish is gray-brown with ten narrow dark brown bands on its body. The median fins are bluish especially over sandy areas where the fish becomes pale. It possesses an unusual gizzard-like stomach to process the algae and sand it ingests.

The doctorfish grows to 13.5 inches (34 cm.) and is found from New England to Rio de Janeiro, including Bermuda.

Philippine Surgeonfish *Acanthurus glaucopareius* Cuvier and Valenciennes

The purple-blue body is strikingly marked with a yellow anal and dorsal fin base and caudal peduncle, a bright orange mark on the dorsal fin, and a white face mark. This hardy aquarium specimen comes from the Indo-Pacific, Hawaii, and Mexico and grows to 7 inches (17.5 cm.). It should be fed fresh protein.

Clown Surgeonfish *Acanthurus lineatus* (Linnaeus)*

This striking fish has a yellow body with 9 to 10 blue stripes edged with brown extending from the head to the dorsal and caudal fins. The belly may vary from red to blue. This Indo-Pacific surgeonfish grows to 8 inches (20 cm.), acclimates well to an aquarium, and feeds on lettuce, brine shrimp, and worms.

Olive Surgeonfish *Acanthurus olivaceous* Bloch and Schneider *

This surgeonfish has two color phases. In one it is generally chocolate brown, and in the other light tan. There is always a short bright orange streak behind the eyes. This fish is found from Indonesia to the Hawaiian Islands and Australia and requires a large tank since it grows to approximately one foot (30 cm.).

Slender-Toothed Surgeonfish *Ctenochaetus strigosus* Quoy and Gaimard*

The body and dorsal and anal fins are dark reddish brown with many horizontal light blue lines. The head is sprinkled with pale red or blue spots. This surgeonfish is found from the Red Sea to the Hawaiian Islands and grows to about 11 inches (27.5 cm.).

Smoothhead Unicornfish *Naso lituratus* (Bloch and Schneider)*
   This fish's body varies from light tan to dull gray-brown becoming lighter ventrally. Its lips are pale red, and a yellow band runs from the mouth to above the eye. The black-edged caudal fin has lobes which become elongated with age. Its most prominent markings are the two brilliant orange spots surrounding the two to three spines on the caudal peduncle.
   It is found in the Red Sea, around Indonesia, the Philippines, offshore of Australia, and Hawaii. This commonly imported species is very hardy and compatible and should be fed lettuce or spinach in addition to fresh protein. It grows large—to 18 inches (45 cm.).

Flagtail (or Blue) Surgeonfish *Paracanthurus hepatus* (Linnaeus)*
   This Indo-Pacific fish is common off of New Guinea, and is also known as the regal or blue tang. Its body is a brilliant ultramarine dramatically marked with two black bands, one curving from the eye to the caudal fin and another below the first running from beneath the third dorsal spine to the caudal fin. The dorsal and caudal fins are edged in black while the rest of the tail fin is brilliant yellow. This commonly imported species is highly compatible with other fishes and feeds on green algae or lettuce and brine shrimp or worms.
   It grows to 10 inches (25 cm.) in length.

Yellow Tang *Zebrasoma flavescens* (Bennett)
   This is one of the hardiest and most frequently imported tangs and is a standout in an aquarium. Those from Hawaii are a brilliant yellow; however, in Polynesia and the Indo-Pacific, they are brownish. When frightened, the yellow tang displays a white streak on its side matching the white spine on the caudal peduncle.
   This species ranges from the East Indies to the Hawaiian Islands and grows to 8 inches (20 cm.) at maturity. It thrives on *Tubifex* worms and a little green algae, lettuce, or spinach.
   (See color photo on back cover.)

---

*Asterisk indicates this species is illustrated in the full-color photographic section of this book.

MOORISH IDOL—Family Zanclidae

Moorish Idol *Zanclus canescens* Linnaeus *

This attractive, exotic looking fish is a standout in any aquarium due to its bold body color patterns and the prominent high dorsal fin which trails behind the tail fin. Its elongated snout is orange above and black below. The compressed body has two broad, vertical black bands and another one on the caudal fin. Between the stripes, the body is white or yellow and often has faint blue trimmings.

Formerly, two species, *Zanclus cornutus* and *Zanclus canescens*, were thought to exist; however, it is now believed that *Zanclus canescens* is the only member. With age it develops protuberances on its forehead and may or may not have small spines at the corners of the mouth.

Ethologist Konrad Lorenz has studied the behavior of these fishes in captivity and reported that brutal fights break out among members of this group. They butt their noses together, whirl about, and bite at each other's dorsal fin. They are compatible and even submissive with fishes, however, outside of the family Zanclidae. The Moorish idols are closely related to the surgeonfishes and often will swim with them in an aquarium. Their pectoral fins, method of propulsion, and certain other anatomical features are similar.

The Moorish idol's body will grow to 7 inches (17.5 cm.). This species is found off Zanzibar, Mauritius, throughout the Indian Ocean, the central Pacific, and near the islands off the Mexican coast. They are common near the Hawaiian Islands and can withstand pollution and salinity changes in their natural environment.

In an aquarium, however, they are extremely fragile fishes and are continually susceptible to bacterial, protozoan, and viral infections. Often very finicky eaters, they feed heartily on *Tubifex* worms or brine shrimp one day and refuse them the next day. Some will even take dry food for a while, and most will sample green algae or lettuce.

They are recommended for the aquarist, only if placed in a tank that has been stable for at least 6 months. Once acclimated, Moorish idols can thrive in an aquarium for years.

Moorish idols are expensive and fragile, but a challenge which can be very rewarding. They require a large tank and should never be kept with fishes that will nip the beautiful dorsal fin. The fin may grow back if attacked, but will probably be crooked.

Do not confuse this elegant fish with the perky little banner fish, *Heniochus acuminatus* (see page 56) or "poor man's" Moorish idol. Although somewhat similar in appearance, the *Heniochus* is hardy and eats readily.

ANEMONEFISHES—Family Pomacentridae

Almost every marine aquarist is familiar with the gaudy, orange and white striped clownfishes darting in and out among deadly anemone tentacles. Their symbiotic relationship with their host has spawned their popular name, anemonefishes. Fishes of the genus *Amphiprion* live among large anemones of the genus *Stoichactis* and *Discosoma*. According to Davenport and Norris (1958), clownfishes obtain their immunity from the anemone by secreting mucus which prevents the anemone's stinging cells (nematocysts) from discharging.

The relationship between these fishes and their host appears to be mutual with each partner benefiting from the presence of the other. The clownfishes seem to gain more, however, since they never are observed in nature without an anemone nearby; and yet, the anemone is frequently seen without a fish. In an aquarium, either one can thrive without the other. The anemonefishes are slow, clumsy swimmers and in their natural environment depend on the anemone for protection from predators. They may forage for food several metres away from their host but will dash back into the tentacles when threatened. The young rarely leave the host, and even the adults settle into the tentacles for the entire night.

Some clownfishes feed on the ejected waste of the anemone and may even obtain nourishment by nibbling on the tentacles. Zooxanthellae, algae which live symbiotically in the anemone's tissues, and nematocysts, the anemone's stinging cells, have been found in the stomachs of clownfishes.

These fishes are often observed rubbing vigorously against the anemone. This theoretically may remove external parasites on the fishes or stimulate and aerate the anemone. In aquariums, certain species of anemonefishes have frequently been observed carrying oversized food to their host, either to feed it or to protect the food from predators, but this rarely if ever has been observed in nature. Certain fishes are highly territorial around their host in captivity; and yet, at sea where anemones are often preyed on by butterflyfishes, the clownfishes are rarely protective.

In an aquarium these small, hardy fishes acclimate well and feed heartily on dry flake food, brine shrimp, *Tubifex* worms, and many forms of fresh protein.

Clownfishes have spawned in captivity many times, but the aquarium-born fishes have never lived to maturity and spawned. See page 134 for information on breeding anemonefishes.

Clark's Anemonefish *Amphiprion clarkii* Cuvier *
(formerly *A. xanthurus* or *A. sebae*)
The body of this species is orangy brown with an orange mouth, belly, pectoral, and ventral fins. Its caudal peduncle is white while the caudal fin is pale yellow. One thick white band encircles the head behind the eyes and another band encircles the middle of the body.

This Indo-Pacific species has spawned in aquariums and grows to 4 inches (10 cm.).

Tomato Anemonefish *Amphiprion frenatus* (Brevoort) *
This fish is found throughout the Indian Ocean and the western Pacific and is frequently imported from the Philippines. The body varies from orange-red to dark brown and bears a thick white bar behind the head. Juveniles have a second white bar behind the first.

These fishes may be aggressive towards their own species, but they are hardy and grow to only 4 inches (10 cm.). They are among the easiest marine fishes to breed.

Clownfish *Amphiprion ocellaris* Cuvier (formerly *A. percula*)*
This sociable, little anemonefish has a brilliant orange body with three white stripes that appear to have been painted on him. The first encircles the head behind the eyes, the second extends from behind the spiny dorsal fin to behind the pectoral fins, and the third encircles the caudal peduncle. The orange fins are rimmed in black and white.

This fish is found in the Indian Ocean and the tropical Pacific and prefers water temperatures between 26°C (78°F) and

---

*Asterisk indicates this species is illustrated in the full-color photographic section of this book.

27°C (80°F). It grows to 4 inches (10 cm.), will take dry food, and is sometimes sensitive when first introduced into an aquarium.

Pink Skunk Anemonefish *Amphiprion perideraion* Bleeker *
The skunk name is derived from the narrow white band which runs along the fish's back (as on a skunk) from the snout to the caudal peduncle. There is also a narrow white bar behind the eyes. The males are distinguished from the females by the bright orange edge on the male's soft dorsal and caudal fin. The females have whitish or translucent fins with no trim.

This species is found in the central Pacific and grows to less than 3 inches (7.5 cm.).

Saddleback Anemonefish *Amphiprion polymnus* (Linnaeus) *
This fish is imported most often from the Philippines and grows to 5 inches (12.5 cm.). Its body is dark orange-brown with a white band encircling the head behind the eyes. A white saddle mark appears on and below the soft dorsal fin. This species can be somewhat sensitive in an aquarium but has spawned in captivity and is compatible with other fishes.

DAMSELFISHES—Family Pomacentridae

Damselfishes are a popular choice for the novice marine aquarist since they are perky, active, and generally colorful specimens. Almost any size tank is suitable, as they are usually less than 6 inches (15 cm.) long. They will feed on most forms of fresh protein and will even relish dry flake food. Damselfishes are recommended for use in "conditioning" the filter bed in a new tank since they are extremely hardy, inexpensive, and less sensitive to toxic nitrites than most fishes. They also appear to be less prone to disease or shock.

Damselfishes are not ideal tankmates, however, since they become highly pugnacious and territorial as they mature. The genus *Dascyllus* includes fishes that are very bossy in an aquarium even though on the reefs they are seen peacefully hovering in cloud-like formations over coral heads. Fishes of the genus *Abudefduf* and *Eupomacentrus* are hardy but scrappy and may eventually grow too large for a small tank. Always supply many hiding places for these fishes to compensate for their territoriality.

The damselfishes exhibit many fascinating behavior patterns. The young are sometimes observed picking parasites from other fishes or inhabiting anemones like their close relatives, the clownfishes.

Blue Damselfish or Blue Devil   *Abudefduf assimilis* (Bleeker) *

This fish is frequently imported from the Philippines. It has a bright blue body with a thin black stripe through the eyes and grows to 4 inches (10 cm.). One of the hardiest and least expensive marine imports, it is excellent for "conditioning" the filter bed in a new tank. Unfortunately, it becomes aggressive and bossy, particularly around its own kind.

Sergeant Major   *Abudefduf saxatilis* (Linnaeus) (see page 97)

These hardy, schooling fishes are abundant on the coasts of tropical America. They are also common in Caribbean waters around wharfs and jetties and in the West Indies.

Since the small body exhibits black and yellow stripes, this fish is sometimes known as the prison fish. It can instantly change, however, to a silver or black fish. In the ocean it is omnivorous, feeding on anemones, algae, small fishes, and invertebrates. In the aquarium it will feed readily on vegetable matter and fresh protein.

It grows to 6 inches (15 cm.). Its eggs are purplish-red and are guarded by the male until hatching. The sergeant major is recommended for beginning aquarists.

Blue Reef Fish   *Chromis coeruleus* (Cuvier and Valenciennes) *

The blue reef fish is another hardy, schooling fish and commonly is found among reefs in the Indo-Pacific and the Red Sea. Unlike most damselfishes its body is thin with a deeply forked tail. This fish is less aggressive than others of its family and grows to 5 inches (12.5 cm.). It should be fed brine shrimp or dry flake food.

Threespot Damselfish   *Dascyllus trimaculatus* Rüppell *

This small, blunt-nosed fish is black with three white spots— one on its head and one on each side of its back. Small specimens are excellent in an aquarium but large ones become scrappy. They are voracious feeders, very hardy, and grow to 6 inches (15 cm.). This species is found in the Red Sea and the Indo-Pacific.

Potter's Angelfish

Rock Beauty

Queen Angelfish juvenile

Queen Angelfish adult

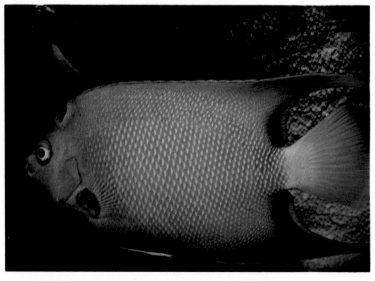

Gray Angelfish

French Angelfish

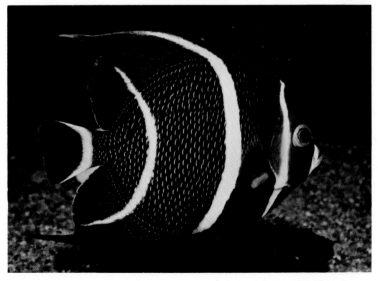

Foureye Butterflyfish

Raccoon Butterflyfish

Black-Backed Butterflyfish

Banded Butterflyfish

Tear Drop Butterflyfish

Vagabond Butterflyfish

Copperbanded Butterflyfish

Longnosed Butterflyfish

Banner Fish

Achilles Tang

Clown Surgeonfish

Olive Surgeonfish

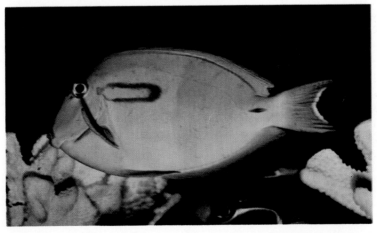

Slender-Toothed Surgeonfish

Smoothhead Unicornfish

Flagtail or Blue Surgeonfish

Moorish Idol

Clark's Anemonefish

Tomato Anemonefish

Clownfish

Pink Skunk Anemonefish

Saddleback Anemonefish

Blue Damselfish or Blue Devil

Blue Reef Fish

Threespot Damselfish

Yellow-Tailed Damselfish

Red Coris Wrasse

Cleaner Wrasse

Rainbow Wrasse

Zebra Lionfish

Triggerfish

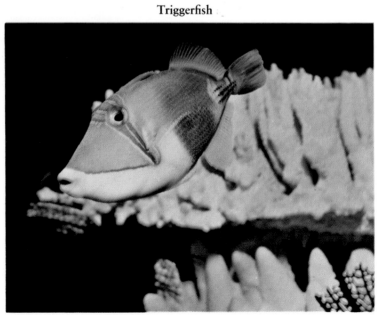

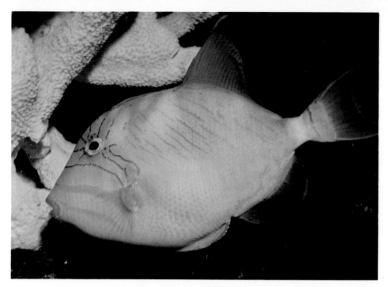

Queen Triggerfish

Clown Triggerfish

Picasso Triggerfish

Fantail Filefish

White-Spotted Puffer

Reticulated Blowfish

Scrawled Cowfish

Smooth Trunkfish

86　Trunkfishes

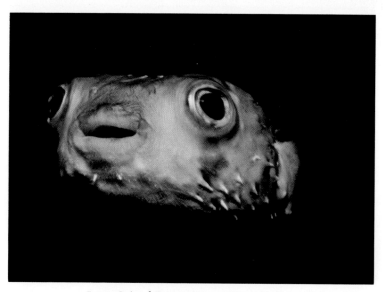

Long-Spined Porcupine or Spiny Puffer

Striped Squirrelfish

Flamefish

Cardinalfish

Mandarin Fish

Round Batfish with Cleaner Wrasses

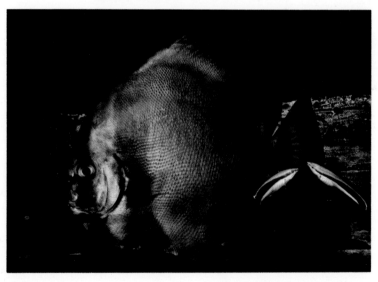

Royal Gramma or Fairy Basslet

Porkfish

French Grunt

Clown Sweetlips

Spotted Hawkfish

Yellowhead Jawfish

Coral Catfish

Spotted Seahorse

Sea Anemone

Flame Scallop

Hermit Crab

Arrow Crab

Banded Coral Shrimp

Sea Star

Sergeant Major

In the ocean it has been observed picking parasites from other fishes. Its color changes during this behavior as well as during mating procedures, etc., and often it is seen turning to an off-white bluish color in seconds. The spawning behavior of *D. trimaculatus* has been greatly studied and is discussed on page 136.

Marine Jewelfish or Yellowtail Damselfish *Microspathodon chrysurus* Cuvier and Valenciennes
In its juvenile stage, this fish is a standout. Its body is dark blue, sprinkled with many brilliant light blue spots, giving it the name of jewelfish. The ventral and anal fins are rimmed with light blue. As the fish ages, the spots disappear and the tail becomes bright yellow.

The marine jewelfish has a good personality and grows to about 6 inches (15 cm.). It is found among coral reefs from the West Indies to Florida and the Gulf of Mexico. Since it feeds on algae and invertebrates in nature, it should be given lettuce and brine shrimp, etc. in the aquarium.

Beau Gregory *Pomacentrus leucostictus* Müller and Troschel
This scrappy little damselfish has a yellow body, a bright blue back, and blue head dotted with brilliant blue spots. Found from

Beau Gregory

New England to Brazil, it is common in Florida among reefs and sandy areas. The beau gregory grows to 4 inches (10 cm.) and is excellent for the novice aquarist.

Yellow-Tailed Damselfish *Pomacentrus melanochir* Bleeker *
This damselfish has a deep royal blue body with a yellow tail. It grows to 3 inches (7.5 cm.) and is found in the waters of Indonesia and commonly among the reefs of Sri Lanka (Ceylon). This species is less likely to fight with its own kind if a large group is in the same tank rather than only a few specimens.

WRASSES—Family Labridae

More than 600 species of wrasses can be found among tropical reefs and in temperate waters. They vary in size from a 3-inch (7.5 cm.) long specimen of the genus *Labroides* to those of the genus *Cheilinus* which grow to a length of 10 feet (3 metres). The wrasses are often vividly colored and usually exhibit a variation in shade between male and female as well as juvenile and adult. Large colorful fishes are usually males while smaller, duller ones may be male or female. They possess a wide range of

Spanish Hogfish (with Cleaner Wrasse)

body shapes but usually are cigar-like with well developed canine teeth.

Certain wrasses, such as *Coris gaimard*, frighten and go into shock easily. When disturbed, they dive under the sand and may emerge only once or twice a week. Eventually they may die from starvation. It is best to introduce them to the aquarium with most of the room lights out and to keep the tank dark until the following day.

The wrasses have interesting sleeping positions. Some sleep buried in the sand while others sleep in coral crevices. Certain wrasses, like the bluehead, *Thalassoma bifasciatum*, secrete a mucous cocoon around themselves. When sleeping or in shock, many lie on the top of the sand on their sides. They may appear dead, but their gill movements are visible. Do not poke a sick or frightened fish in this position or you may drive him deeper into shock.

Almost all wrasses are carnivorous and thrive on *Tubifex* worms or brine shrimp in captivity. At sea they feed on mussels, snails, crabs, and small invertebrates, and some even bite off pieces of coral branches in order to reach the invertebrates. Young blueheads *(Thalassoma bifasciatum)*, young Spanish hogfishes *(Bodianus rufus)*, and members of the genus *Labroides* remove and ingest parasites from the body surfaces, mouth, and gills of larger fishes.

Cleaner wrasses *(Labroides dimidiatus)* are excellent aquarium additions because of the fascinating cleaning service they provide and due to their hardy, active nature. The larger wrasses do not make good tankmates since they use their sharp teeth to attack other fishes, including their own species. Some, such as the razorfishes, may even bite when handled.

Spanish Hogfish *Bodianus rufus* Linnaeus

Spanish hogfishes grow to 3 feet (1 metre) in length but do well in an aquarium when small. They are found in deep water from the West Indies to the Florida Keys. In juveniles the upper anterior two thirds of the body is blue or plum colored while the rest is yellow.

In nature the adults feed on crabs, sea urchins, and other invertebrates, while the young clean ectoparasites from other fishes. Once adjusted to captivity, they feed well and can be started on fresh protein.

Red Coris Wrasse *Coris gaimard* Quoy and Gaimard *

This brilliantly colored little fish is found from Micronesia and Polynesia to the Hawaiian Islands. It undergoes a dramatic color change from the juvenile to adult stage. Juveniles are imported most frequently and are bright orange-red with five white spots rimmed in black. Adults are reddish-brown with small blue spots on the body, green or blue lines through the eyes, and a yellow tail fin.

Coris gaimard grows to 16 inches (40 cm.) in length and tends to go into shock easily. If frightened, it will dive under the sand or lie on the surface as if dead. If it adjusts to captivity, it will thrive on fresh protein and be fairly hardy.

Bird Wrasse *Gomphosus varius* Lacépède

This wrasse grows to 10 inches (25 cm.) and ranges throughout the Indo-Pacific including Hawaii. Fishes of this species are characterized by the elongated jaws which are used to reach into crevices for food. The green or blue color phase indicates the mature male and the brown phase the female. This species is very hardy and can be fed brine shrimp, *Tubifex* worms, and algae or lettuce.

Cleaner Wrasse *Labroides dimidiatus* Bleeker *

This small blue and black striped wrasse is well known for its doctoring abilities. In the ocean it can be seen entering the

Bird Wrasse

mouths and gills of groupers and moray eels, while in the aquarium it will be seen picking parasites and dead tissue from many species of fishes. It generally sleeps in coral crevices or on the surface of the sand.

Its coloration is very similar to the neon goby *(Gobiosoma oceanops)* and to the sharp-toothed blenny *(Aspidontus taeniatus)*. The latter imitates the wrasse's cleaning behavior but rips off pieces of flesh instead of parasites.

The cleaner wrasse ranges from the Pacific to the Indo-Pacific and the Red Sea and grows to 4 inches (10 cm.). It is a very hardy fish and should be fed brine shrimp or small worms. This fish is highly recommended for any aquarium.

Rainbow Wrasse *Thalassoma lucasanum* (Gill)*

The common name stems from the gaudy horizontal bands on the wrasse's head and body. Its dorsal fin is black with a yellow stripe at its base from the head to the caudal peduncle. Below this is a thick brownish-black band. Ventrally, the body is lined with a yellow stripe, a pink one, and a white belly.

This wrasse grows to 5 inches (12.5 cm.) and inhabits tide pools off the Pacific coast of Mexico and in the Gulf of California. It should be fed brine shrimp, *Tubifex* worms, or chopped shrimp in an aquarium.

Green Parrot Wrasse *Thalassoma lunare* (Linnaeus)

This gaudy wrasse has a green body with vertical red lines through each scale and reddish-purple stripes on its face. The pectoral fins are reddish-purple and edged in light blue. The inner part of the caudal fin is yellow.

This wrasse inhabits the Red Sea and the tropical Indo-Pacific. It is capable of surprisingly fast bursts of speed although it is normally a slow swimmer. Although carnivorous, it will take dried food and can grow to 10 inches (25 cm.). This species is hardy, lively, and highly recommended.

LIONFISHES OR SCORPIONFISHES— Family Scorpaenidae

These spectacular-looking fishes are highly venomous, with poisonous glands at the base of their sharp dorsal fin. They can inflict extremely painful wounds and must be handled with great care. Tankmates must be chosen cautiously since lionfishes prefer live fishes for food. They should be fed live guppies or goldfishes at first and then weaned to fresh protein dropped into the water.

These striking fishes have loose skin, or dermal flaps, which move with the water currents and serve as camouflage. Their pectoral fins are oversized and are used to herd prey into position for attack. The lionfishes generally are very hardy and tame in an aquarium and can be kept safely with fishes their size.

The deadly stonefishes are also members of this family, but are definitely not recommended for the aquarist.

Zebra Lionfish *Dendrochirus zebra* Quoy and Gaimard *
In this genus the membrane between the pectoral rays extends almost to their tips, whereas in *Pterois* (see below) the rays are separated most of the way. The pectoral fins do not reach the caudal peduncle. The body is reddish with two to three vertical dark bars on the head and six to seven on the trunk. The soft dorsal, caudal, and anal fins bear rows of dark spots.

This hardy species grows to 8 inches (20 cm.) and inhabits shallow reefs from the Red Sea to Polynesia.

Whitefin Lionfish *Pterois radiata* Cuvier and Valenciennes
The body is reddish-brown with narrow, vertical white lines. The pectoral fins are extremely large and lack spots, and the

head lacks distinct stripes. A distinguishing feature is the caudal peduncle which displays two white horizontal lines.

This species is very dangerous, slightly more fragile than *Pterois volitans* (see below) and does not take dead protein as readily. It is found in the Indo-Pacific and the Red Sea and grows to 10 inches (25 cm.). This is a fairly hardy species which can do well in an aquarium.

Hawaiian Lionfish *Pterois sphex* (Jordan and Evermann)
This commonly imported lionfish is found off the Hawaiian Islands. The reddish-brown body is marked with vertical white bands, and the fins are spotted. The head does not have any distinct stripes. This species grows to about 10 inches (25 cm.).

Lionfish *Pterois volitans* (Linnaeus)
This is the most frequently imported lionfish even though it is the largest member of the family and grows to 15 inches (37.5 cm.) in length. The reddish head and body are lined with alternating brown and white vertical bands while the soft dorsal, caudal, and anal fins bear rows of black spots. The pectoral and ventral fins display larger spots.

This species is found in the Red Sea, along the east coast of Africa, and in the Indian Ocean. It is hardy, eats small fishes, and can be weaned to dead protein. Avoid contact with the spines since they are highly venomous.

TRIGGERFISHES—Family Balistidae

This group of fishes derives its name from the fact that its first dorsal spine can be erected and locked into place by its second dorsal spine. The purpose is not defensive. The fish swims into a coral crevice at night and erects its spines to lodge it there while it sleeps.

These exotic looking fishes are brightly colored and exhibit intricate patterns. Often such patterns on the head make the mouth appear oversized. Most members of this group require a large tank since they grow to 2 feet (60 cm.) in length. The family contains approximately 30 species, and they are found in almost all shallow tropical waters, with only a few inhabiting temperate waters.

Red-Toothed Triggerfish

The triggerfishes are slow swimmers and can make a grunting sound using their swim bladders. They are carnivorous and will eat pieces of fishes, shrimp, crabs, molluscs, echinoderms, or other fresh protein. Their powerful jaws are used to crush shellfish and coral. Although these fishes are very hardy, they are extremely aggressive and great care should be taken in selecting tankmates. At sea, they are found singly or in pairs.

Certain triggerfishes found in the Pacific Ocean are poisonous if eaten, even though they are edible in other parts of the world. The hypothesis is that the flesh becomes toxic when the triggerfishes feed on other fishes that have consumed toxic blue-green algae.

Triggerfish *Rhinecanthus verrucosus* (Linnaeus)*
This hardy, common triggerfish grows to 8 inches (20 cm.) and is found from the Red Sea to Malaysia, Indonesia and the Hawaiian Islands. This species is very similar in appearance to the Picasso triggerfish *(Rhinecanthus aculeatus)* (see page 106).

The body is grayish tan with a white stripe edged in orange from the snout to the pectoral fins. There are several blue, yellow, and brown stripes through the eyes to the pectoral fins and a large dark patch from in front of the dorsal to the anal fin. This is a good aquarium specimen which feeds readily.

Queen Triggerfish *Balistes vetula* Linnaeus *

This beautiful fish is common from Florida to the Caribbean and ranges from New England to Brazil. Its body is yellow to blue-gray and streaked with thin blue lines. Two bright blue lines run across the snout, while several others pass through the eyes. The caudal peduncle as well as the dorsal, anal, and caudal fins are edged in a brilliant blue. As the fish matures, the dorsal and caudal fins become elongated.

In nature, adults feed on sea urchins and other invertebrates. This species grows to 16 inches (40 cm.) and generally is compatible with other fishes except other triggerfishes in the genus *Balistes*. *Vetula* means "old wife" and is sometimes used as the common name for this fish.

Clown Triggerfish *Balistoides conspicullum* (Bloch and Schneider)*

A healthy clown triggerfish is generally worth $100 to $250. It is a fantastic, gaudy, aggressive treasure, decorated with whitish polka dots on its belly and a brilliant orange mouth.

It is believed that small specimens are found in deep waters of the Indo-Pacific, and due to this inaccessibility are rarely imported. When they reach 6 to 8 inches (15 to 20 cm.), they can be found near reefs and are more available to divers. Since they can grow to 20 inches (50 cm.) they need a large tank and in spite of their peaceful nature generally are not kept with other fishes.

Black Durgeon *Melichthys niger* (Bloch)

This circumtropical species grows to 14 inches (35 cm.) or more and is common in the deep water of outer reefs all over the world. Its body and fins are black and sometimes tinted with dark green. The dorsal and anal fin bases are pale blue. This triggerfish is omnivorous and in nature feeds on algae or floating plant material.

Black Triggerfish *Melichthys ringens* Osbeck

This circumtropical species is as aggressive as it is common all over the world and should be kept with fishes at least as large as it is. Its body is uniformly brownish black with blue-white lines at the base of the dorsal and anal fins. It grows to 20 inches (50 cm.) and is often confused with *Melichthys niger*.

Humu-Humu-Nuku-Nuku-A-Puaa

Red-Toothed Triggerfish *Odonus niger* Rüppell

This species is generally the least aggressive of the triggerfishes and is very hardy. Found throughout the tropical Indo-Pacific, it is common around Sri Lanka (Ceylon). Its entire body is green while the teeth are red. It grows to 20 inches (50 cm.) in length.

Picasso Triggerfish *Rhinecanthus aculeatus* (Linnaeus)*

The grayish body is decorated with many abstract designs and colors which make it look like it might have been painted by Picasso and accounts for this fish's popular name. Between mid-body and the anal fin there is a large dark area interrupted by four or five oblique white bands. There are four blue stripes between the eyes and three from the eye to the pectoral base. A yellow-orange band runs from the snout to the pectorals. A distinctive feature of this species is the three rows of strong, recurved spines on the caudal peduncle.

Although this fish grows to 10 inches (25 cm.) it is frequently imported from the Indo-Pacific in a much smaller size. The smaller specimens are generally less aggressive than the large ones.

Humu-Humu-Nuku-Nuku-A-Puaa *Rhinecanthus rectangulus* (Bloch and Schneider)

This triggerfish grows to 9 inches (22.5 cm.) and is found off of Africa, in the Red Sea, and the Indo-Pacific, including the

Hawaiian Islands. It is very similar to the Picasso triggerfish but has slightly different markings. The body is yellow dorsally and white ventrally and bears a dark brown angular band from above the eye through the pectoral base to the anal fin base. Also, a yellow-edged dark triangular area extends forward from the caudal peduncle. This species may be aggressive towards its tankmates.

FILEFISHES—Family Monocanthidae

This group of fishes derives its name from the file-like texture of its skin which is abrasive and scaleless. In some species, however, the skin is velvety. The filefishes resemble the trigger-fishes in some particulars, as they have a compressed body and a small mouth. In place of the trigger, however, they have one strong dorsal spine and sometimes a rudimentary one over the eyes. These spines and the ventral spine are used to lodge the fish into coral. Another unique feature of this group is the replacement of the pelvic fins with a pelvic flap.

Certain filefishes are common among beds of seaweed. They are capable of staying vertical among the plants and changing their colors for camouflage.

The filefishes are notoriously hard to feed. Basically herbi-vorous, they relish green algae, spinach, or lettuce. They may also eat coral polyps, sponges, and small crustaceans, such as brine shrimp. The food must be small, and the fishes must be allowed a long time to feed. It is best to start them on newly hatched brine shrimp. Filefishes have a docile nature and do best if kept with two or three others of their own species.

Scrawled Filefish *Aleutera scripta* (Osbeck)

The body of this species has highly variable coloration but is generally blue-gray or olive-brown with black spots and blue-green lines. The young adapt their body color to the surround-ings and drift head down to mimic blades of grass.

At sea, this species feeds on algae, seagrass, anemones, small fishes, and shrimp. In an aquarium it can be fed small live fishes or ground shrimp.

The scrawled filefish is found in all tropical seas and can grow to 36 or 40 inches (90 or 100 cm.) long. A small specimen may be kept in an aquarium, but should have a tank of its own or it may attack its tankmates.

Fantail Filefish *Pervagor spilosoma* Lay and Bennett *
This fish derives its name from its bright, orange-red, fan-shaped tail which bears a black border. Its body is gold with black spots, and its head has dark stripes. The tail is normally kept folded unless the fish is frightened. It is then spread like a fan, and the dorsal spine is erected.

This odd-looking fish is found from Indonesia to the Hawaiian Islands and grows to 6 inches (15 cm.) in length.

PUFFERS—Family Tetraodontidae

The strange-looking puffers are well known for their ability to inflate their bellies with air or water when alarmed. Among sharpnose puffers (formerly Canthigasteridae), the body is slightly compressed, and the snout is narrow and elongated. Among other puffers the snout is blunter and the body rounder. The tail is curved forward to the side.

These fishes are generally seen swimming over sandy bottoms or reefs, and they feed on crustaceans and molluscs. In an aquarium, puffers are colorful but aggressive. They should be fed fresh protein such as shrimp, clams, worms, or brine shrimp since they are carnivores.

White-Spotted Puffer *Arothron meleagris* (Schneider)*
This species grows to 10 inches (25 cm.) and has a dark body with small white spots. When frightened, it may emit a toxic mucus which can be lethal in an aquarium. It is found off Hawaii, but is uncommon.

Reticulated Blowfish *Arothron reticularis* (Bloch)*
The body of this fish is gray-brown above and white below, with many longitudinal dark stripes curving around the pectoral fins, eyes, and mouth. The back and caudal peduncle bear white spots among dark reticulated lines.

This species is similar to *Arothron meleagris* except for the reticulated color pattern. It inhabits the tropical Indo-Pacific and grows to 17 inches (42.5 cm.) in length.

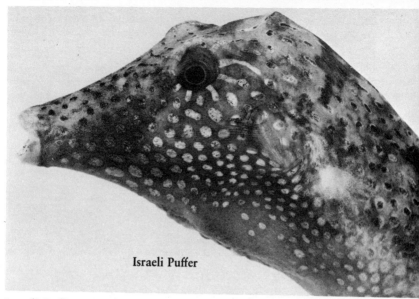

Israeli Puffer

Israeli Puffer *Canthigaster cinctus* (Richardson)

This sharpnose puffer has two dark bands over the back and sides and one over the eye and the caudal peduncle. The rest of its body is tan and white with orange or brown spots and several stripes running through the eyes.

The Israeli puffer is found from the tropical Indo-Pacific to the Hawaiian Islands and grows to 5 inches (12.5 cm.) in length.

Hawaiian Sharpnose Puffer *Canthigaster jactator* (Jenkins)

This small, common puffer is found off the coasts of the Hawaiian Islands. It has white spots on a dark body, but not on any of the fins. This is a hardy species which feeds well on brine shrimp and grows to about 3 inches (7.5 cm.) in length.

TRUNKFISHES—Family Ostraciidae

Trunkfishes are small, odd-looking animals with bodies resembling armor. Their box-like shells consist of hexagonal bony plates with holes for the mouth, eyes, fins, and vent. The body color varies with maturity, and there is a difference in coloration between the sexes. Similar to seahorses, the trunkfishes swim

---

*Asterisk indicates this species is illustrated in the full-color photographic section of this book.

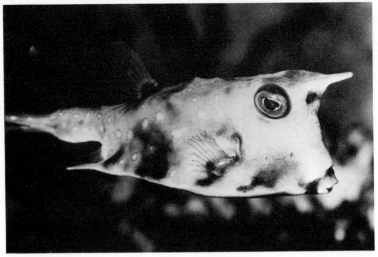

Long-Horned Cowfish

awkwardly, using their dorsal and anal fins. The pectorals are constantly moving and help water pass through the immobile gill cover.

Cowfishes derive their name from the two horns on their heads. They have an excellent personality and become extremely tame. Unfortunately many of these fishes in nature inhabit bays and, therefore, are likely to be carrying parasites or bearing skin infections.

In spite of being highly compatible with other species, cowfishes should be kept alone to avoid infestation. An additional reason for keeping them isolated is that certain species of trunkfishes can discharge a toxic mucus when frightened. This poison may kill all animals in the aquarium. In spite of this toxin, trunkfishes are often roasted and eaten by people in the West Indies and the Indo-Pacific.

Trunkfishes have tiny mouths and a large appetite and require a great quantity of small-sized food, such as brine shrimp. At sea, they feed on crustaceans and worms on the ocean floor.

Scrawled Cowfish *Acanthostracion quadricornis* (Linnaeus)*

This fish's body is pale gray-brown with blue spots and markings which extend onto the caudal peduncle and fin. There are usually blue bands between the eye and mouth as well as a long blue ventral stripe. The markings are highly variable, however, and some specimens show almost none. The parallel stripes below the eye are usually visible.

This species grows to 18 inches (45 cm.) and ranges from New England to Brazil. In the ocean, it feeds on sponges, anemones, crabs, other invertebrates, and marine plants. In the aquarium, it should be fed brine shrimp and worms.

Smooth Trunkfish *Lactophrys triqueter* (Linnaeus)*

This trunkfish lacks spines and has a black body covered with small white spots. The lips and the bases of the dorsal and pectoral fins are black.

This fish grows to 12 inches (30 cm.) and is found from New England and Bermuda to Brazil. In nature, it feeds on a variety of invertebrates (worms, crab, shrimp, etc.) and exposes burrowing animals by ejecting water from its mouth at the sand. This species apparently secretes a toxic substance when excited, but is otherwise a hardy aquarium fish.

Long-Horned Cowfish *Lactoria cornuta* (Linnaeus)

This species inhabits tropical waters all over the world and is common along the Great Barrier Reef of Australia where it is found in shallow coral pools. Its popular name is derived from the long horns on top of its head. The body is a yellowish-tan with light blue spots except on the plain yellow belly.

The maximum size of this fish is 10 to 16 inches (25 to 40 cm.), but it is generally about 2 inches (5 cm.) when imported. This cowfish is prone to skin infections but is otherwise hardy.

PORCUPINEFISHES AND BURRFISHES— Family Diodontidae

These fishes derive their name from the sharp spines which cover their bodies. The beak-like mouth, small head, and thick body resemble those of the puffer. By gulping air or water the fish can inflate its body, making the spines jut out at right angles. The burrfish has permanently erect spines even when the body is not inflated. These fishes are commonly dried and sold as a tourist oddity or souvenir.

There are from 9 to 15 species of porcupinefishes and burrfishes throughout the tropical seas of the world. They inhabit the

Spiny Boxfish

warm, inshore waters such as ports, shallow reefs, and beaches. Some of these fishes grow too large for the aquarium, and all require protein, such as worms or shellfishes, for food. In their native environment, porcupinefishes use their strong jaws to feed on molluscs. In the aquarium, they eat readily and eject water at the sand in order to uncover and capture their prey.

Spiny Boxfish *Chilomycterus schoepfi* (Walbaum)
This small burrfish has a greenish to brownish body with wavy lines and a large dark spot above and behind the pectoral fins, but no small dark spots on the body. The short, stubby spines are erect and immobile.

This species is found in tropical seas and sometimes wanders north to Cape Cod in the summer. It grows to 10 inches (25 cm.) in length.

Long-Spined Porcupinefish or Spiny Puffer *Diodon holacanthus* Linnaeus *
The body is light greenish brown dorsally and white ventrally with a large brown band between the eyes and extending beneath them. Another dark band lies behind this one on the back,

and a third surrounds the dorsal fin. Additional dark spots are scattered over the upper part of the head and body. The fins are light yellowish and lack spotting.

This species grows to 20 inches (50 cm.) and is found among reefs or mangrove channels throughout the tropical seas of the world. In nature, its diet consists of sea urchins, molluscs, and crabs.

Porcupinefish *Diodon hystrix* Linnaeus
This species is found in all tropical seas including waters around Florida and the Gulf Stream. The body is pale green-brown with small black spots dorsally, and is solid white ventrally. There are no large, distinct brown blotches as in *Diodon holacanthus*. The spines are normally laid back against the body, but jut out when the fish is inflated.

D. *hystrix* grows to 3 feet (1 metre) and in nature feeds on crabs, molluscs, and sea urchins.

SQUIRRELFISHES—Family Holocentridae

The squirrelfishes, also known as soldierfishes because of their spines, are basically nocturnal, solitary, and shy. To compensate for their shyness, provide adequate cover for them in the aquarium. Most members have stocky, red bodies which are accentuated by a pair of oversized, squirrel-like eyes.

Their distribution is circumtropical, but they are most common in shallow waters from Florida to Brazil. These fishes can grow to 1 to 2 feet (30 to 60 cm.) in length.

Captive squirrelfishes may prey on smaller tankmates and will generally accept most forms of fresh protein.

Striped Squirrelfish *Adioryx xantherythrus* (Jordan and Evermann)*
This attractive species is found in the tropical Pacific from Samoa to the Hawaiian Islands and grows to 7 inches (17.5 cm.). The body is silvery red with pale pink or blue stripes on the sides.

Longjaw Squirrelfish *Holocentrus ascensionis* (Osbeck)
This species is silvery red with faint stripes on its sides. The tail is deeply forked, and the fish grows to 1 to 2 feet (30 to 60 cm.)

Longjaw Squirrelfish

in length. This is a common Florida species and ranges from New York and Bermuda to Brazil.

Like all members of the genus *Holocentrus*, this squirrelfish has a voracious appetite and should not be kept with small fishes. In an aquarium, pieces of fresh protein should be dropped into the water to feed them since they will only accept moving food. Few will feed on matter lying on the bottom.

CARDINALFISHES—Family Apogonidae

Cardinalfishes are generally bright red or copper colored and 4 inches (10 cm.) or less in length. Native to shallow water tropical seas, these nocturnal fishes require much cover and are fond of hiding in shells or sponges.

They have a large head, eyes, and mouth and should not be kept with small fishes. They can, however, coexist with angelfishes, damselfishes, and gobies. The large mouth is used to carry eggs for incubation or protection, by either the male or the female, depending on the species. This method of reproduction eventually may enable cardinalfishes to be bred in captivity.

They can be fed small live fishes or fresh protein such as worms, raw beef, or shrimp.

Flamefish *Apogon maculatus* (Poey)*
This fish's popular name stems from its bright red coloration. It is distinguished by a dark spot at the base of the second dorsal fin, one on the caudal peduncle, and one behind the eyes.

It ranges from Florida to Brazil and occasionally is seen further north. This species grows to 4 inches (10 cm.) in length and is a mouthbreeder.

Cardinalfish *Apogon orbicularis* Cuvier and Valenciennes*
This species grows to 4 inches (10 cm.) and is found in the Indo-Pacific. The greenish-brown body bears a wide dark band in the mid-region. Posterior to this, the body and caudal peduncle are speckled with reddish spots.

This cardinalfish is distinctive in that it often hovers motionless in an aquarium. It is very hardy and has spawned frequently in captivity.

DRAGONETS—Family Callionymidae

Dragonets are small, elaborately colored bottom fishes that generally inhabit shallow bays and deep water in temperate and tropical seas. They are scaleless, and generally possess two elongated dorsal fins with weak spines. They also have pre-opercular spines.

Strong sexual differences exist between members of this family with males being more brightly colored, having larger bodies, longer snouts, longer caudal and first dorsal fins, and more brightly ornamented membranes.

Mandarin Fish *Synchiropus splendidus* (Herre)*
The mandarin is a dazzling jewel in any aquarium. Its body is orange with black-edged green wavy bands on body and fins. Between these bands are spots of a similar color. The head is green above, yellow below, and displays thin black-edged blue stripes.

Mandarin fishes are very hardy, curious, and compatible in a

---

*Asterisk indicates this species is illustrated in the full-color photographic section of this book.

well established aquarium. They are slow eaters, feeding off the bottom or swimming up to the food, which should be brine shrimp or *Tubifex* worms.

Males of this species cannot be kept with other males, but a male and one or more females will be peaceful. These fishes are found mainly in the Indo-Pacific and grow to only 3 inches (7.5 cm.) in length.

GOBIES—Family Gobiidae

Approximately 400 species of gobies are distributed throughout the world making this the largest family of fishes that are primarily marine. Some are found in deep water while others inhabit coral reefs or inshore tidepools.

Gobies have a separate first dorsal fin. The ventral fins under the pectorals resemble a suction cup which enables the tiny fishes to withstand waves lashing against their tidepools.

In an aquarium, these fishes will attach to the glass or to rocks and wait for food to come to them. They feed on crustaceans, worms, algae, and detritus.

Most gobies are between 2 and 4 inches (5 to 10 cm.) in length, but the smallest and lightest fishes known today also belong to this group. Some gobies from the Philippines, Marshall Islands and Samoa are only $\frac{1}{2}$ inch (12.5 mm.) long at maturity, and weigh only 2 milligrams.†

Gobies are commonly involved in a mutual relationship with an invertebrate. The California arrow goby, *Clevelandia ios*, inhabits a hole in the mud flats with a pea crab, and a burrowing worm, *Urechis*. The southern California blind goby, *Typhiogobius californiensis*, depends upon the ghost shrimp, *Callianassa affinis*, for its survival. The shrimp digs a burrow in the gravel which the goby then inhabits. It is also possible that the shrimp creates a current of water laden with microscopic food for the goby. Similarly, in the Indo-Pacific, gobies of the genus *Smilogobius* guard the entrance of a burrow maintained by snapping shrimp.

---

† The *Guinness Book of World Records* reports that 17,750 of these dwarf gobies weigh one ounce.

Neon Goby

Neon Goby *Gobiosoma oceanops* Jordan

The body has a blue stripe edged in black running from the snout to the tail. This fish inhabits the Caribbean and grows to 3.5 inches (9 cm.) in length. It cleans external parasites from larger fishes in the same manner that the cleaner wrasse (*Labroides dimidiatus*) performs this service in the Indo-Pacific.

This goby has spawned in captivity, but the fry have not been raised successfully. See page 138 for information on breeding neon gobies. This hardy, compatible fish will feed on dry flake food and fresh protein.

Catalina or Blue-Banded Goby *Lythrypnus dalli* Gilbert

These brightly colored little fishes are orange-red with several blue bands on the sides of the bodies. They are common in rock crevices in water more than 20 feet (6 metres) deep along the California coast and grow to approximately 2 inches (5 cm.).

In an aquarium, they prefer water temperatures of 18°C (65°F) or less and feed on newly hatched brine shrimp.

(See color photo on front cover.)

BATFISHES—Family Platacidae

The majestic-looking juveniles have long dorsal and anal fins and a light brown or gray body with three dark vertical stripes. As they age, the bands are lost and the fins shorten, making the body appear rounder.

Batfishes are excellent aquarium specimens if kept away from fishes that might nip their beautiful fins. Highly resistant to disease, they relish worms, brine shrimp, and even dry food. They become extremely tame and can thrive in captivity for many years. Although small specimens are frequently imported, batfishes grow very quickly to a maximum of 26 inches (65 cm.).

They are imported from the shallow, quiet tropical waters of the Indo-Pacific.

Round Batfish *Platax orbicularis* (Forskål) *

This is the most commonly imported species of batfish. It is very hardy and will accept fresh protein and dried food. The fins are not as elongated as other species, and the body is a light brown with two or three dark brown, vertical bands.

This fish is found in the Red Sea and the Indo-Pacific and grows to 1 to 2 feet (30 to 60 cm.) in length.

Orange-Ringed Batfish *Platax pinnatus* (Linnaeus)
This is the most spectacular of the group but also the least common and least hardy. It requires a large tank and live worms. Its body is chocolate brown with three diffuse dark bands, and is almost completely outlined with a thin, brilliant orange margin. Members of this species grow to at least one foot (30 cm.) in length.

Longfinned Batfish *Platax tierra* (Forskål)
This Indo-Pacific batfish is hardy and will feed on fresh protein and sometimes dried food. The dorsal, anal, and ventral fins are extremely elongated and narrow, and the body is gray-brown with three dark vertical bands in young specimens. Members of this species may attain a length of 2 feet (60 cm.).

SPADEFISHES—Family Ephippidae

These fishes are found in schools off both coasts of the tropical Atlantic. They are related to the batfishes, but unlike them have a deep indentation between the first and second dorsal fins. The juveniles have laterally compressed, dark bodies with five or six vertical bands. With age, the body becomes lighter in color and the stripes disappear. These fishes grow to 3 feet (1 metre) in length and are silver at maturity.

The spadefishes feed on sponges, coelenterates, algae, and molluscs in their natural environment and can be fed worms, brine shrimp, and lettuce in the aquarium.

Atlantic Spadefish *Chaetodipterus faber* (Broussonet)
The small juveniles of this species are solid black and resemble plant debris. As they grow, they become silvery gray with dark vertical bands. They can attain a length of 3 feet (1 metre) and are found from New England to Brazil. In nature, the adults school and feed on sponges, worms, and algae.

Spadefish or John Dory *Tripterodon orbis* Playfair
This rare spectacular fish is found off the coast of Africa. It is

closely related to the batfish, *Platax*, and grows to 30 inches (75 cm.) and 20 pounds. The body is silvery and orbicular with indistinct bands in the young. Several dorsal spines are elongated.

GROUPERS AND SEABASSES—Family Serranidae

About 500 species of groupers and seabasses are to be found in tropical and temperate seas, and they vary in size from 1 inch to over 4 feet (2.5 to 120 cm.). Their coloration can change instantly, making species identification difficult. Those in tanks are so intelligent and friendly that they will recognize their owner.

These hardy, colorful carnivores have large mouths and sharp teeth and should not be kept with smaller fishes and must be provided with a large tank. Sluggish unless attacking prey, they will eat chunks of fresh protein.

Black Grouper *Cephalopholis argus* Bloch and Schneider
The color of this grouper is highly variable but generally is brown or black with blue spots on the head, body, and fins. This species is found throughout the central Indo-Pacific and grows to 18 inches (45 cm.).

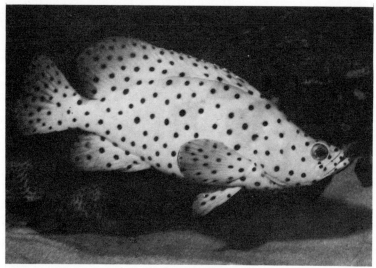

Pantherfish

Pantherfish *Chromileptis altivelis* (Cuvier and Valenciennes)

This fish is gray-brown with round black spots on the body, head, and fins. These spots become smaller and more numerous with age. Its head is undersized relative to its body, and the mouth and pectoral fins are large.

The pantherfish grows to 26 inches (65 cm.), is peaceful and hardy, but should not be kept with small fishes.

Golden Striped Grouper *Grammistes sexlineatus* (Thunberg)

This Indo-Pacific grouper grows to 10 inches (25 cm.) and has lived as much as 12 years in an aquarium. Its body is dark brown with short white or yellow dashes which become numerous lines with age. This species is popular, hardy, and feeds voraciously, but may eat small tankmates.

BASSLETS—Family Grammidae

Royal Gramma or Fairy Basslet *Gramma loreto* Poey *

The basslets are a family of small, colorful reef fishes which are closely related to the groupers and seabasses (Family Serranidae).

The royal gramma is brilliantly colored with the anterior half of its body being violet and the posterior half being orange-yellow. A black spot adorns the dorsal fin.

It is found in caves or under ledges in shallow or deep water off Bermuda, the West Indies, and in the western Caribbean. This solitary fish grows to 3 inches (7.5 cm.) and feeds on small crustaceans or fish larvae at sea. In the aquarium, it is very hardy and usually feeds well.

GRUNTS—Family Pomadasyidae

The grunts belong to the same family as the sweetlips (see page 122) and are closely related to snappers (Lutjanidae). By grinding their pharyngeal (throat) teeth and amplifying the sound with their swim bladder, they produce a noise which gives them their common name.

During the day they hover in dense aggregations or schools

over reefs, and at night they disperse to feed individually over sand and grassy areas. At sea, they feed on bottom invertebrates and in an aquarium will eat almost any protein food.

Porkfish *Anisotremus virginicus* (Linnaeus)*
This deep-bodied fish is striped with silvery blue and yellow horizontal bands. It has a wide black bar from the top of its head through the eyes to the mouth. There is a similar band posterior to the first from the first dorsal spine to the pectoral fins, which are yellow.

The young have a yellow head and white body with two horizontal black stripes. They often are observed picking ectoparasites from other fishes.

The porkfish grows to one foot (30 cm.) long and inhabits the reefs from Florida and Bermuda to Brazil. This hardy species feeds on small invertebrates in the ocean and fresh protein, such as worms or brine shrimp, in an aquarium.

French Grunt *Haemulon flavolineatum* (Desmarest)*
This species exhibits two color phases. The more common one consists of a golden body with silver-blue stripes and yellow fins. In the pale color phase, the body is yellow with silver-white stripes. On the upper part of the body the lines are horizontal, whereas on the lower and mid-regions they are oblique.

This fish, which grows to one foot (30 cm.), is found from South Carolina to Brazil, and is most common among the reefs of Florida and the West Indies. French grunts drift in large schools by day and feed on molluscs, crustaceans, and some small fishes at night. They accept animal protein in an aquarium, are very hardy, and do well with their own species.

It is common to see two of these fish push against each other with their mouths open. It is unknown whether this is sexual or territorial display.

SWEETLIPS—Family Pomadasyidae

Clown Sweetlips *Plectorhynchus chaetodontoides* (Lacépède)*
This is the most commonly imported species in this group. The common name is derived from the large white spots which cover the chocolate brown head, body, and fins.

This fish grows to 18 to 36 inches (45 to 90 cm.) in length and inhabits waters of the Red Sea, Indonesia, and the Philippine Islands. In an aquarium, it is compatible, somewhat delicate, and can be fed live protein and plant food.

HAWKFISHES—Family Cirrhitidae

Hawkfishes are quiet bottom fishes which inhabit coral reefs. They perch on the top of coral or cling to it with their pectoral fins. Small fishes and invertebrates are what they generally feed on.

Spotted Hawkfish *Cirrhitichthys aprinus* (Cuvier)*
This tropical Indo-Pacific species has distinctive blueish tufts on each dorsal spine. The body, which varies from white to reddish tan, has large reddish brown spots or blotches on its sides and fins.

Spotted Scat

It grows to 4 inches (10 cm.) in length, is hardy, and feeds well on brine shrimp and *Tubifex* worms. It is highly compatible, except with members of its own species.

SCATS—Family Scatophagidae

This small family consists of about six species which are found mainly in bays and river mouths of the Indo-Pacific. They may adapt to either fresh- or salt-water aquariums.

The body is blue-gray or greenish gray with many dark spots. The juveniles are attractive due to their orange-red coloration, and are compatible and active.

Scats grow to 12 inches (30 cm.) and feed on spinach, lettuce, and pieces of fish or beef. In the ocean, these fishes are found near sewer outlets and feed on decaying refuse. They are commonly seen schooling in southeast Asian ports.

Spotted Scat *Scatophagus argus* (Gmelin)
This species has variable coloration. Generally the adult body is silver-green with dark spots. Juveniles are orange-red on the dorsal surface.

In an aquarium, the spotted scat grows to about 4 inches (10 cm.), while in nature it may reach a foot (30 cm.) in length. This is a very hardy fish which does well in an aquarium in a group and thrives on green algae or lettuce and protein.

JAWFISHES—Family Opistognathidae

The jawfishes obtain their common name from their oversized mouth which some species use for breeding purposes. Their head and eyes are also large and their body is elongated.

This family is known for its custom of building burrows in the sand and lining them with stones or shell fragments. Tail first they enter their home and cautiously poke their head outside. They will defend their dwelling vigorously against even their own species.

Yellowhead Jawfish *Opistognathus aurifrons* (Jordan and Thompson)*

This popular, hardy, aquarium species has a pale gray-blue body, a yellow head, and black spots on the chin. It grows to 4 inches (10 cm.), is a mouthbreeder, and should be supplied with enough sand and small stones for a burrow. Found from the West Indies to Florida, it inhabits shallow water.

CATFISHES—Family Plotosidae

These fishes have elongated bodies with pointed tails. They possess four pairs of barbels and dorsal and pectoral fins with serrated spines.

Coral Catfish *Plotosus anguillaris* (Bloch)*

The body and head of this species are gray-black with two horizontal white stripes running from the snout to the tail fin. On the chin are four pairs of barbels.

This Indo-Pacific species grows to 30 inches (75 cm.) or less, is very hardy, and eats readily. Young fishes should be kept as a school. Be cautious when handling this species since the pectoral spines are venomous.

SEAHORSES AND PIPEFISHES— Family Syngnathidae

These small fishes have segmented bodies encased in bony plates. Although they have long tubular snouts, and small anal and pectoral fins, they lack spinous dorsal and ventral fins.

The seahorse has a head, neck, and chest resembling a horse, and possesses a prehensile tail used in anchoring it to seaweed, etc. In an aquarium, sticks or coral branches should be provided.

The pipefish is long and slender and has a caudal fin in place of the prehensile tail. Its body may be solid colored, mottled, or vividly striped.

The syngnathids are generally camouflaged among turtle

grasses in shallow bays, although some species inhabit coral reefs or floating masses of sargassum seaweed.

They should be kept in a tank of their own or with other slow-eating fishes since they feed very cautiously and require almost a constant supply of brine shrimp. Dwarf seahorses or juveniles require newly hatched brine shrimp and may feed for up to 10 hours a day. Generally only live food is accepted. Large sea-horses have a life expectancy of 2 to 3 years, while dwarfs have a shorter lifespan.

The spawning of seahorses in aquariums is not uncommon. See page 137 for information on breeding these fishes.

Spotted Seahorse *Hippocampus sp.* Bleeker*
The color of this species varies from gray to yellow, brown,

A decorative branch creates depth and attractiveness, and offers suitable cover for fishes such as seahorses. Clean it regularly.

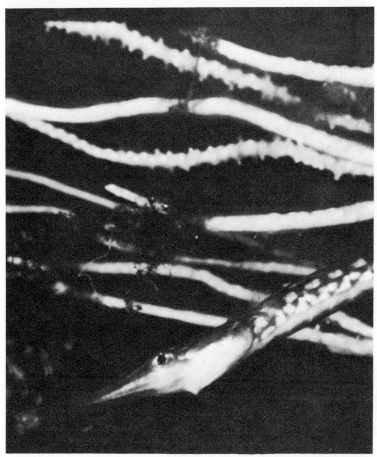

Pipefish

or black. It usually has black bands or spots on the body, and sometimes white spots are evident.

This hardy fish is found off of Zanzibar, India, Indonesia, the Philippines, Japan, New South Wales, Polynesia, and Hawaii. It grows to 8 inches (20 cm.) and is frequently imported.

Dwarf Seahorse *Hippocampus zosterae* Jordan and Gilbert

Dwarf seahorses grow to only 1 to 2 inches (2.5 to 5 cm.) in length. They breed most readily of all seahorses in captivity, are hardy, and can be fed newly hatched brine shrimp. They are mostly found off of Florida, in the Gulf Coast, and in the Caribbean.

Northern Pipefish *Syngnathus fuscus* Storer
This pipefish inhabits shallow water from Halifax to North Carolina, and grows to 7 inches (17.5 cm.).

MORAY EELS—Family Muraenidae

The moray eel, in spite of its looks and reputation, is generally shy and retiring. It will defend its territory, however, and bite if provoked. It possesses very powerful jaws, usually has long canine teeth, and often a brilliant and distinctively marked body.

These secretive eels hide in rock and reef crevices and are nocturnal. As scavengers and predators, they feed mainly on fishes and grow to 4 or 5 feet (120 or 150 cm.) in length.

White-Spotted Moray Eel *Gymnothorax meleagris* (Shaw and Nodder)
This Indo-Pacific moray eel is common among shallow reefs. It is brown with numerous small white spots on the head and body and grows to about 3 feet (90 cm.) in length.

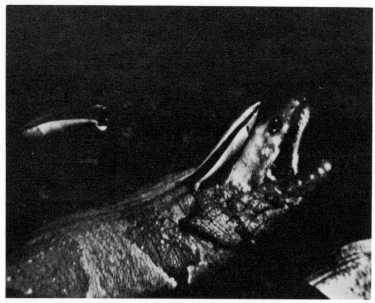

Moray Eel and Cleaner Wrasses

8. Marine Invertebrates for the Aquarium

When hobbyists set up their first marine aquarium, few think of keeping invertebrates; and yet, these can be the most interesting, colorful, inexpensive, and hardy acquisitions available. There appears to be a much lower incidence of disease among captive invertebrates than among marine fishes. Some require special feeding procedures, but others do not require feeding at all since they filter nourishment directly from the water.

Many aquarists advise against mixing invertebrates and fishes in one tank, but the author has never encountered problems with this. It is simply a matter of selecting compatible species.

FEEDING

Some invertebrates, such as the banded coral shrimp, are fed as easily as fishes and will thrive on *Tubifex* worms. Others, such as anemones and certain crabs, must have the food placed near them.

Filter feeding invertebrates, such as scallops and live coral, strain nourishment directly from the water and may not need any additional food. They will thrive, however, if at least once a week they receive a supplement of liquid food (e.g. Liquifry or liquefied minced clams) or live infusoria. It also is simple to raise your own brine shrimp and, as soon as they hatch, feed them to the invertebrates.

It is safest to feed these filter feeders in an aerated mixing bowl or plastic bucket rather than in the tank, since the fine food particles could easily foul the water. Be cautious about any food left on your specimens when they are returned to the main tank, or the fishes may peck at the food and injure the invertebrates.

SEA ANEMONES*

These "flower animals" belong to the phylum *Cnideria* and the class *Anthozoa*. The beautiful sea anemones look like plants —they exhibit a wide variety of brilliant colors and shapes—but are animals and make an excellent addition to a marine aquarium. Slow-moving, they consist of an oral disc surrounded by waving tentacles, a trunk or body stem, and a basal disc which adheres to the sand or the sides of the tank.

Anemones are known for their nematocysts, or stinging cells, which are used to capture prey and fend off predators. These cells contain a thread with a miniature barb on the end. When the cell is stimulated by a fish brushing against it, it fires the barb into the victim's skin and this injects a poison. The combined impact of hundreds of cells exploding at the same time paralyzes the prey.

Anemones are not a threat to their tankmates since healthy fishes instinctively know to maintain a safe distance. Certain fishes have a symbiotic relationship with the anemone and live safely among the tentacles. (See ANEMONEFISHES, page 61.)

When purchasing or collecting an anemone, choose one that is fully inflated unless it has just been fed. The tentacles should not be deflated and wrinkled at the tips, and there should not be excessive mucus around the base. Be careful not to tear the basal disc by which it adheres when removing it from the substrate.

In an aquarium, anemones need strong aeration, good water circulation, high water quality, and strong light, under which they usually thrive. Many anemones contain zooxanthellae, algae living symbiotically in the tissues, which require light for photosynthesis. They are assumed to provide nourishment for their host, but anemones can live without them. These animals are also capable of living in a tank without their partners, the anemonefishes.

Anemones are carnivores and will thrive on worms, scallops, pieces of dead fish, clams, or other protein dropped directly on the tentacles.

Their reproductive process may begin by a small piece of tissue breaking off and developing into a new animal. They are also thought to reproduce by releasing sperm and eggs into the water, or by internal fertilization.

---

*Asterisk indicates this species is illustrated in the full-color photographic section of this book.

Yellow Coral

CORAL

The coral animal is a compound polyp, closely related to the sea anemone. It lives in colonies consisting of many thousands of individual flower-like structures. As humans grow flesh over an inner skeleton of bones corals grow thin tissue over a skeleton of lime. The coral sold in aquarium shops for decoration is merely the skeleton which remains after the animal dies.

The polyps contain nematocysts, and all reef-building corals contain zooxanthellae. Feed the coral in your tank by placing it in a bowl with newly hatched brine shrimp, Liquifry, or other liquid food, such as pulverized clams. Many types of coral remain deflated during the day and only inflate and feed at night. They should be allowed at least an hour to feed and can be fed every two days.

Coral reproduces in a manner similar to sea anemones.

FLAME SCALLOP*

The brilliant red flame scallop belongs to the phylum *Mollusca* which includes the clam, snail, chiton, octopus, squid, etc. This bivalve generally lies motionless on the surface of the sand, but is capable of great bursts of speed if threatened. It propels itself through the water by snapping the shells closed repeatedly, causing a jet propulsion effect.

The flame scallop, found in tropical waters, is a filter feeder. In the ocean, it feeds on bacteria, algae, protozoans, and invertebrate larvae. In an aquarium, some specimens can live for many months by straining organic matter from the water. Since the amount of nutrients varies from tank to tank, however, it is best to give these animals special attention. They will thrive if fed every other day in an aerated bowl filled with brine shrimp larvae or liquefied minced clams. Allow them at least one hour to feed.

HERMIT CRABS*

Hermit crabs are an excellent addition to a marine aquarium since they are extremely hardy scavengers. They are known for their habit of seeking out empty snail shells to carry on their backs for protection. Unlike other crabs, the hermit lacks the protective exoskeleton on its abdomen and therefore, must hide it in a shell.

They never kill an occupant in order to secure a shell, but always seek empty ones. When their current shell is outgrown, they search for a larger one.

Many hermit crabs have a symbiotic relationship with anemones and are known to physically remove one or more from the substrate and place it on their shell. These crabs are a comical sight carrying their top-heavy shells overgrown with waving anemones.

In an aquarium, hermit crabs can be fed shrimp, clams, fishes, *Tubifex* worms, or other protein. Since they are scavengers and feed on left-over debris or dead fish on the surface of the sand, they reduce the risk of the water becoming polluted from decaying matter. They generally are nocturnal, grow very rapidly, and should be supplied several empty shells of various sizes.

ARROW CRAB *Stenorhynchus seticornis* (Herbst)*

The arrow crab is an odd-looking, fairly hardy marine crustacean. It has an elongated head, striped body, and long spider-like legs. Feed it *Tubifex* worms, scallops, fish or other protein.

Crabs, in particular arrow crabs, often lose one or more legs in fights with their tankmates. A new leg will start to regenerate almost immediately and will be complete after several moults. This is not a problem if these crabs are kept with docile fishes and compatible invertebrates.

BANDED CORAL SHRIMP *Stenopus hispidus*
(Olivier)*

These shrimp are decorated like red and white candy canes and are also known as barber-pole shrimp. In the ocean, their long white antennae wave from among coral crevices to attract moray eels, groupers, etc. for cleaning. The shrimp picks parasites from the surface of these fishes. In an aquarium, it rarely cleans its tankmates, but is highly territorial. Never put two coral shrimp in one tank or they will fight until one or both are killed.

The shrimp, like the crab, has a firm skeleton to provide support for its body. Since this skeleton cannot grow, the shrimp periodically must moult. This generally happens at night when the outer shell is cast off and is replaced by a new softer skeleton. The tissues rapidly take up water, the new skin hardens, and growth stops until the next moult. Don't be surpised to see two lifelike shrimp in your tank some morning. The old skeleton is a carbon copy of the live shrimp and appears very real.

These animals will feed heartily on *Tubifex* worms, scallops, pieces of fish, etc.

SEA STARS*

The sea stars belong to the phylum *Echinodermata* which means "spiny skinned." The adults are radially symmetrical, generally have five body segments, and no distinct head. They have a water vascular system consisting of a canal encircling the mouth and extending into each of the five sections. This system is used to operate the sucker-like tube-feet which aid in locomotion and in adherence to the substrate.

Sea stars are carnivorous and feed on coral, molluscs, worms, crustaceans, and other echinoderms. Be careful when selecting invertebrate tankmates for these animals. The sea star feeds on shellfish by clasping the shell with its tube-feet and forcing the shell open. It then everts its stomach, digests the animal, and withdraws the stomach back into its own body. In an aquarium, sea stars should be fed fish, clams, or mussels.

9. Breeding Marine Fishes

Until recent years almost no marine fishes had ever been bred in captivity. Now reports are coming in from all over the world of successful matings in aquariums. This exciting stage of the marine aquarist's hobby, however, is still in its infancy. Juveniles born in aquariums have yet to be raised to maturity and successfully bred themselves. At a time when environmentalists are balking at the great numbers of marine fishes and invertebrates being taken from the ocean, we should be trying harder than ever to unlock the secrets of breeding marine fishes. Not only will the aquarist have an assured supply of fishes and invertebrates in the future, but these specimens will be much hardier and healthier than "wild" ones which must adapt to a new environment.

ANEMONEFISHES (Family Pomacentridae)

Courtship and Nest Building
Anemonefishes seem to form permanent pairs that are capable of spawning at monthly intervals throughout the year. One fish will posture to the other by dipping a dorsal fin towards its mate. They may then swim side by side leaning dorsally or ventrally, touching bellies, and nearly rolling over. A smooth, flat rock surface next to their anemone is usually chosen as a nest site and cleaned by the male several days prior to spawning. The anemone's tentacles frequently touch the nesting area.

Egg Laying and Care
Oddly enough, a significant number of spawnings occur within 6 days before or after a full moon. The female deposits 300 to 700 eggs with a visible white ovipositor, and the male then swims over the eggs fertilizing them. He also mouths and fans them for the 6- to 7-day incubation period. He is commonly observed biting the substrate and removing dead eggs from the nest as

well as nibbling the tips of the anemone's tentacles sweeping over the eggs. The female forages for food while the male cares for the nest. Often it is left completely unattended. The eggs generally hatch after dark on the seventh day of the incubation period.

Breeding Anemonefishes in Captivity

At least six species of anemonefishes have been bred in aquariums with *Amphiprion ocellaris* (formerly *A. percula*) and *Amphiprion perideraion* being the easiest to breed. Unfortunately these aquarium-born fishes have yet to be successfully bred.

Selecting a Pair

To complicate the problem, it is difficult or impossible to determine the sex of most marine fishes. The pink skunk anemonefish, however, can be sexed 100 per cent of the time. The male's soft dorsal and caudal fins are edged in bright orange. The females have whitish or translucent fins with no trim. For other species, you generally can assume that a large, heavier-bodied fish (female) chasing a smaller fish (male) without hurting it is likely to be a mated pair.

Sometimes *A. ocellaris* can be sexed by observing the width of the white bands. In males, the central band is wide and points toward the head, and the band on the caudal peduncle is slightly wider than the female's. In females, the central band's anterior edge is blunt, and the band itself is narrower than the male's. If you are unable to sex the species you wish to breed, purchase four or five individuals to insure obtaining a pair.

Breeding Tank

Although *A. ocellaris* has spawned in a 15-gallon (60-litre) aquarium, a large, uncrowded tank should be used for breeding experiments. For large species, such as *A. clarkii*, a 100-gallon (400-litre) tank is recommended. For anemonefishes the water temperature should be about 28°C (82°F) to 29°C (85°F), and their natural host anemone should be kept in the aquarium. Place a large, flat rock next to the anemone.

Rearing the Young

As soon as the eggs have hatched, the young should be removed to a 5- to 10-gallon (20- to 40-litre) rearing tank. This will prevent their being eaten by the adults, and insure that their specialized food does not pollute the main aquarium. The fry can be collected by suspending a strong light at the corner of the tank. They will be attracted to the light and then can be siphoned out.

The major problem with rearing the larval and juvenile fishes is food. Some fishes have been successfully raised on liquefied dry flake food for the first three days or so of life. By then they are large enough to consume brine shrimp nauplii (larvae) with the liquefied food as a supplement. Since young fishes grow very rapidly, they need almost a continual supply of food at first. In addition to the brine shrimp nauplii, they feed on algae and microscopic organisms on the sides of the tank. If you live near the ocean, you can add "living rocks" to the aquarium. These are pieces of rock or coral which are overgrown with many forms of marine life which the newly hatched fishes can eat.

Do not assume your young fishes are dead if you do not see them swimming around in the evening. In the early stages of development, some species lie on the bottom at night.

DAMSELFISHES (Family Pomacentridae)

Courtship

The threespot damselfish, *Dascyllus trimaculatus*, has been greatly studied and is representative of this group of fishes. It appears to mature at the age of one year and pairs off at this time. In the initial courtship display, the pair face each other and swim in circles with much fin quivering and body shaking. This species may change from black to a powdery bluish-white during the posturing phase. A stone, shell, or coral surface is chosen for the nest site.

Egg Laying and Care

These fishes are capable of spawning as often as three times a month. The female's short, white ovipositor protrudes through the vent and deposits a row of 5 to 12 eggs. The male swims over them, fertilizing them. This process is repeated until 20,000 to 25,000 adhesive, elliptical eggs have been laid in small clusters. The male guards the eggs for the 4- to 5-day incubation period.

SEAHORSES AND PIPEFISHES (Family Syngnathidae)

Courtship and Egg Laying

Dwarf Seahorse *Hippocampus zosterae*

The breeding period for this species is from late winter through autumn. Courtship involves both sexes swimming back and forth, circling each other, and eventually clasping tails. One of the fishes will quiver from tail to head and the other will copy this behavior. The female inserts her ovipositor in the male's kangaroo-like pouch and deposits the eggs. They are fertilized by the male while in the pouch and carried for the 10-day incubation period.

When the eggs hatch, 25 to 55 miniature young seahorses are expelled from the pouch by convulsive movements of the male's body. He is again capable of breeding within 2 to 3 days. Dwarf seahorses reproduce frequently in aquariums, and even their young can reproduce in captivity. The juveniles should be fed brine shrimp nauplii.

Other Seahorse Species

The larger seahorses breed in the same manner as the dwarfs, but have an incubation period of up to 6 weeks and commonly produce 100 or more young with each spawning. The expulsion of the young from the male's body may take up to 4 days. If the water temperature is around 29°C (85°F), they can hatch approximately two broods each month except from early winter to mid-winter. These fishes do not breed as readily as the dwarfs in captivity.

Pipefishes

The spawning of pipefishes is similar to that of seahorses except that the male pipefish has a series of ventral flaps in place of a brood pouch, and the spawning period is late spring to early summer.

GOBIES (Family Gobiidae)

Nest Building and Egg Laying

Neon Goby *Gobiosoma oceanops*

   Neon gobies have spawned in aquariums and are representative of this family. They intimately pair off better than any other salt-water species and spawn in the spring and autumn. They make a nest together by shovelling sand with their fins from underneath a piece of coral. They also may select a clean surface for a nest, such as inside a shell. The female deposits about 100 eggs which the male fertilizes. Both fishes guard the eggs during the 2-week incubation period.

Sexing Neon Gobies

   These fishes are sexually mature at about 1.3 inches (3.25 cm.) and are difficult to sex. The males generally are larger with longer fins and brighter colors. The black horizontal stripe on the side of the male's body rises distinctly on the caudal fin. The female's stripe turns downward or is straight at this point.

SCIENTIFIC NAME INDEX

Abudefduf assimilis, 64
Abudefduf saxatilis, 64
Acanthostracion quadricornis, 110
Acanthurus achilles, 57–58
Acanthurus chirurgus, 58
Acanthurus coeruleus, 57
Acanthurus glaucopareius, 58
Acanthurus lineatus, 58
Adioryx xantherythrus, 113
Aleutera scripta, 107–108
Amphiprion clarkii, 62, 135
Amphiprion frenatus, 62
Amphiprion ocellaris, 62–63, 135
Amphiprion perideraion, 63, 135
Amphiprion polymnus, 63
Anisotremus virginicus, 122
Apogon maculatus, 115
Apogon orbicularis, 115
Arothron meleagris, 108
Arothron reticularis, 108
Aspidontus taeniatus, 101
Balistes vetula, 105
Balistoides conspicullum, 105
Bodianus rufus, 99, 100
Canthigaster cinctus, 109
Canthigaster jactator, 109
Centropyge flavissimus, 48–49
Centropyge loriculus, 49
Centropyge potteri, 49
Cephalopholis argus, 120
Chaetodipterus faber, 119
Chaetodon capistratus, 53
Chaetodon kleini, 53
Chaetodon lunula, 53
Chaetodon melannotus, 53
Chaetodon miliaris, 54
Chaetodon ocellatus, 54
Chaetodon striatus, 54
Chaetodon unimaculatus, 54
Chaetodon vagabundus, 54
Chelmon rostratus, 55
Chilomycterus schoepfi, 112

Chromileptis altivelis, 121
Chromis coeruleus, 64
Cirritichthys aprinus, 123–124
Clevelandia ios, 116
Coris gaimard, 99, 100
Ctenochaetus strigosus, 58
Dascyllus trimaculatus, 64–65, 136
Dendrochirus zebra, 102
Diodon holocanthus, 112–113
Diodon hystrix, 113
Forcipiger flavissimus, 55
Gobiosoma oceanops, 101, 118, 138
Gomphosus varius, 100
Gramma loreto, 121
Grammistes sexlineatus, 121
Gymnothorax meleagris, 128
Haemulon flavolineatum, 122
Heniochus acuminatus, 56, 61
Hippocampus sp., 126–127
Hippocampus zosterae, 127, 137
Holocanthus ciliaris, 49
Holocanthus isabelita, 49–50
Holocanthus tricolor, 49, 50
Holocentrus ascensionis, 113–114
Labroides dimidiatus, 38, 100–101, 118
Lactophrys triqueter, 111
Lactoria cornuta, 111
Lythrypnus dalli, 118
Melichthys niger, 105
Melichthys ringens, 105
Microspathodon chrysurus, 97
Naso lituratus, 59
Odonus niger, 106
Opistognathus aurifrons, 125
Paracanthurus hepatus, 59
Pervagor spilosoma, 108
Platax orbicularis, 118–119
Platax pinnatus, 119
Platax tierra, 119

Plectorhinchus chaetontoides,
   122–123
Plotosus anguillaris, 125
Pomacanthus arcuatus, 50
Pomacanthus imperator, 50
Pomacanthus paru, 50
Pomacanthus semicirculatus,
   51
Pomacentrus leucostictus,
   97–98
Pomacentrus melanochir, 98
Pterois radiata, 102–103
Pterois sphex, 103
Pterois volitans, 103
Rhinecanthus aculeatus, 104,
   106

Rhinecanthus rectangulus, 106
Rhinecanthus verrucosus, 104
Scatophagus argus, 124
Stenopus hispidus, 133
Stenorhynchus seticornis, 132
Synchiropus splendidus,
   115–116
Syngnathus fuscus, 128
Thalassoma bifasciatum, 99
Thalassoma lucasanum, 101
Thalassoma lunare, 101
Tripterodon orbis, 119–120
Typhiogobius californiensis,
   116
Zanclus canescens, 60
Zebrasoma flavescens, 56, 59

POPULAR NAME INDEX

(Italic page numbers indicate pictures)

Achilles Tang, 57–58, *72*
Arrow Crab, *95*, 132
Atlantic Spadefish, 119
Banded Butterflyfish, 54, *69*
Banded Coral Shrimp, *96*, 133
Banner Fish, 56, 61, *72*
Beau Gregory, 97–*98*
Bird Wrasse, 100, *101*
Black-Backed Butterflyfish, 53, *69*
Black Durgeon, 105
Black Grouper, 120
Black Triggerfish, 105
Blue Angelfish, 49–50
Blue-Banded Goby, *see* Catalina Goby
Blue Damselfish, 64, *78*
Blue Devil, *see* Blue Damselfish
Blue Reef Fish, 64, *79*
Blue Surgeonfish, 59
California Arrow Goby, 116
California Blind Goby, 116
Cardinalfish, *88*, 115
Catalina Goby, 118
Clark's Anemonefish, 62, *76*
Cleaner Wrasse, 38, *81*, 100
Clownfish, 62–63, *77*
Clown Surgeonfish, 58, *73*
Clown Sweetlips, *91*, 122
Clown Triggerfish, *83*, 105
Common Butterflyfish, 54
Copperbanded Butterflyfish, 55, *71*
Coral, *131*
Coral Catfish, *93*, 125
Diagonal Butterflyfish, *55*
Doctorfish, 58
Dwarf Seahorse, 127, 137
Fairy Basslet, *90*, 121
Fantail Filefish, *84*, 108
Flagtail Surgeonfish, 59, *75*
Flame Angelfish, 49

Flamefish, *88*, 115
Flame Scallop, *94*, 131–132
Foureye Butterflyfish, 53, *68*
French Angelfish, 50–51, *67*
French Grunt, *91*, 122
Golden Striped Grouper, 121
Gray Angelfish, 50, *67*
Green Parrot Wrasse, 101
Hawaiian Lionfish, 103
Hawaiian Sharpnose Puffer, 109
Hermit Crab, *95*, 132
Humu-Humu-Nuku-Nuku-A-Puaa, *106*–107
Israeli Puffer, *109*
John Dory, *see* Spadefish
Koran Angelfish, *51*
Lemon Butterflyfish, 54
Lemon Peel, 48–49
Lionfish, 103
Longfinned Batfish, 119
Long-Horned Cowfish, *110*, 111
Longjaw Squirrelfish, 113–*114*
Longnosed Butterflyfish, 55–56, *71*
Long-Spined Porcupinefish, *87*, 112
Mandarin Fish, *89*, 115–116
Marine Jewelfish, 97
Moorish Idol, 60–61, *75*
Moray Eel, *128*
Neon Goby, *117*, 118
Northern Pipefish, 128
Olive Surgeonfish, 58, *73*
Orange-Ringed Batfish, 119
Pantherfish, *120*, 121
Philippine Surgeonfish, *57*, 58
Picasso Triggerfish, *84*, 106
Pink Skunk Anemonefish, 63, *77*, 135
Pipefish, *127*
"Poor man's" Moorish Idol, *see* Banner Fish

Porcupinefish, 113
Porkfish Grunt, *90*, 122
Potter's Angelfish, 49, *65*
Queen Angelfish, 49, *66*
Queen Triggerfish, *83*, 105
Raccoon Butterflyfish, 53, *68*
Rainbow Wrasse, *81*, 101
Red Coris Wrasse, *80*, 100
Red-Toothed Triggerfish, *104*, 106
Reticulated Blowfish, *52*, 108
Rock Beauty, 50, *65*
Round Batfish, *89*, 118
Royal Gramma, *90*, 121
Saddleback Anemonefish, 63, *78*
Scrawled Cowfish, *86*, 110–111
Scrawled Filefish, 107–108
Sea Anemone, *94*, 130
Sea Star, *96*, 133
Sergeant Major, 64, *97*
Slender-Toothed Surgeonfish, 58, *74*
Smoothhead Unicornfish, 59, *74*
Smooth Trunkfish, *86*, 111

Spadefish, 119–120
Spanish Hogfish, *99*, 100
Spiny Boxfish, *112*
Spiny Puffer, *87*, 112
Spotted Hawkfish, *92*, 123–124
Spotted Scat, *123*, 124
Spotted Seahorse, *93*, 126–127
Striped Squirrelfish, 113
Sunburst Butterflyfish, 53
Tear Drop Butterflyfish, 54, *70*
Threespot Damselfish, 64, *79*, 97, 136
Tomato Anemonefish, 62, *76*
Triggerfish, *82*, 104
Vagabond Butterflyfish, 54–55, *70*
Whitefin Lionfish, 102–103
White-Spotted Moray Eel, 128
White-Spotted Puffer, *85*, 108
Yellowhead Jawfish, *92*, 125
Yellow-Tailed Damselfish, *80*, 98
Yellow Tang, 59, *back cover*
Zebra Lionfish, *82*, 102

SUBJECT INDEX

Acanthuridae, 56–59
aeration, 19
aggression and compatibility, 26–27, 30, 47
anatomy (diagram), 46
anemonefishes, 61–63, 134–136
angelfishes, 48–51
Apogonidae, 114–115
aquarium maintenance, 31–32
Argulus, 43
Balistidae, 103–107
basslets, 121
batfishes, 118–119
Benedenia melleni, 42–43
breeding, 134–138
    anemonefishes, 134–136
    damselfishes, 136
    gobies, 138
    seahorses and pipefishes, 137
burrfishes, 111–113
butterflyfishes, 52–56
buying healthy fishes, 28–30
Callianassa affinis, 116
Callionymidae, 115-116
cardinalfishes, 114-115
catfishes, 125
Chaetodontidae, 48–56
Cirrhitidae, 123-124
cleaner wrasse, 38, 43, 100–101
collecting, economics of, 11
compatibility chart, 47
conditioning period, 27–28
copper test, 36–37
Cryptocaryon irritans, 38–39
damselfishes, 63–64, 97–98, 136
Diodontidae, 111–113
disease, 35–47
disease symptoms, 37
dragonets, 115–116
Echinodermata, 133
Ephippidae, 119–120
equipment, aquarium, 13–19
feeding, 30–31, 129
filefishes, 107–108

filter, outside, 17–18
filter, subsand, 15, 16
"fin rot", 40
formalin bath, 36
gas bubble disease, 43–44
"gill disease," 39–40
glossary, 8
gobies, 116–118, 138
Gobiidae, 116–118
Grammidae, 121
groupers, 120–121
grunts, 121–122
hawkfishes, 123–124
heating the aquarium, 21–23
Holocentridae, 113–114
hydrometer, 33
Ichthyophonus hoferi, 42
Ichthyophthirius, 38
invertebrates, for aquarium, 129–133
    feeding, 129
isolation tank, 23, 35–36
jawfishes, 124–125
lionfishes, 102–103
Lorenz, Konrad, 60
Lymphocystis, 41
Monocanthidae, 107–108
moray eels, 128
Muraenidae, 128
nematocysts, 61, 130
nitrite level and testing, 27–28, 29, 34
Oodinium ocellatum, 39–40
Opistognathidae, 124–125
Ostraciidae, 109–111
parasites, 37–38
    bacterial infections, 40–41
    crustaceans, 43
    fungus, 42
    protozoans, 38–40
    viral infections, 41
    worms, 42–43
pea crab, 116
pH, 33–34

pipefishes, 125–128, 137
planning and choosing marine fishes, 26–27
Platacidae, 118–119
Plexiglas, 12–14
Plotosidae, 125
Pomacentridae, 61–64, 97–98
Pomadasyidae, 121–123
popeye, 44
porcupinefishes, 111–113
preventive medicine, 35–37
puffers, 108–109
salinity, 33
"salt water ich," 38–39
Scatophagidae, 124
scats, 124
Scorpaenidae, 102–103
scorpionfishes, *see* lionfishes
sea anemones, 61, 130
seabasses, 120–121
seahorses, 125–128, 137
sea water, collecting, 21
sea water, synthetic *vs.* natural, 20–21
Serranidae, 120–121
setting up a successful aquarium, 24–25

spadefishes, 119–120
squirrelfishes, 113–114
stress, 35
surgeonfishes, 56–59
sweetlips, 122–123
Syngnathidae, 125–128
tangs, *see* surgeonfishes
tank
    capacity for maintaining fish, 27
    hood and light, 14–15
    kind of sand, 15–16
    larger sizes preferred, 14
    sterilization, 44–55
temperature, 33
Tetraodontidae, 108–109
triggerfishes, 103–107
trunkfishes, 109–111
tuberculosis, 40–41
Tubifex worms, 30, 60, 132, 133
ultraviolet light, for purification, 18
Urechis, 116
Vibrio, 40
"white spot disease," 38–39
wrasses, 98–102
Zanclidae, 60–61
zooxanthellae, 130, 131